Letters to Young People

LETTERS TO YOUNG PEOPLE

A Spiritual Legacy For A New Generation

EDITED BY
Susan Hodges Bryant
&
M. Darrol Bryant

A NEW ERA BOOK
PARAGON HOUSE
NEW YORK

First edition, 1989
Published in the United States by
Paragon House
90 Fifth Avenue
New York, NY 10011
Copyright © 1989 by
All rights reserved. No part of this book may be reproduced, in any form, without written permission from the publishers, unless by a reviewer who wishes to quote brief passages.
Manufactured in the United States of America

Library of Congress Cataloging-in-Publication Data
Letters to young people.
  "A new ERA book."
  1. Religions—Juvenile literature. 2. Youth—Religious life. 3. Human ecology—Religious aspects—Juvenile literature. I. Bryant, M. Darrol. II. Bryant, Susan Hodges.
BL92.L48   1988   291'.088055   88-6008
ISBN 0-913757-72-1

The paper used in this publication meets the minimum requirements of American National Standard for Information Sciences—Permanence of Paper for Printed Library Materials, ANSI Z39.48-1984.

CONTENTS

FOREWORD vii
Emir Calluf 3
Truneh Wolde Selassie 7
Piara Singh Sambhi 11
Jocelyn Helleq 13
Wilbagedara Dhammika 17
Purushottam L. Bhargava 19
Dr. Inamullah Khan 23
Ingrid Nyborg-Fjellander 25
Anonymous 29
Miriama Widakowich Weyland 31
Anonymous 33
M. C. Bhandari 35
Dr. Sayi Matha Siva Brinda Devi 37
M. J. Chidzungu 39
Mrs. N. R. Sinari 41
Nevzat Erkmen 43
Al-Abdin 45
Carmen Dragonetti 47
Lelitto Arganando 49
Dr. M.M.J. Marasinghe 51
Franklin G. O'Connor 53
Mitra Uncle 57
Kwan Soh Ko 61
Jean Head 63

John T. Mathew   65
V. Ramakrishnan   67
Teh Thean Choo   69
Reverend Clifton V. Bullock   73
Susheela Raghavan   77
Kitan   79
A. Pundara   81
Anil Sooklal   83
Julix Busto   85
Mohan Sharma   87
Epitacio Torres   89
Dohan Effendi   91
Dr. I. C. Sharma   93
Erik   95
Gebre Michael Felema   97
Reverend Teisen Perusat Stork   99
Sister Frances Bernardone Kapouch, IHM   101
Ton-heu Fok   103
Geddes MacGregor   105
R. A. Sinari   107
Dr. Narayan H. Samtani   109
Walerian Skomka   111
Anonymous   113
Andrew Gonzalez   115
Peggy Morgan   119
Irene M. Kessy   121

FOREWORD

These letters are gifts to a younger generation. Written by mothers, fathers, religious leaders, aunts, uncles, scholars, and professional people, they seek to pass their faith and convictions on to those who are the next link in the cycle of life. The authors of these letters are Buddhists, Christians, Hindus, Jews, Muslims, Sikhs, and others whose lives have been shaped by the many different traditions that make up the human family. What the writers all share, despite the differences of faith and culture, is, as one of the letters expressed it, a conviction that "the best we can do is to pass on to the next generation the lessons that life has taught us." The authors select a variety of insights to pass on. Some share their concern with contemporary life and their difficulty with the meaning of their own faith. Others recall the teachings of their tradition that they have found to be spiritually ennobling and helpful. Still others rejoice at "the colors of the rainbow" in nature and in the diversity of traditions, paths, and cultures, reminding their readers of the "codes of conduct" worthy of emulation. All the letters attempt to reach across generations and touch the heart.

A concern for the religious and spiritual welfare of the next generation links these letters by men and women from Africa, Asia, Europe, Latin America, India, and North America. And the letters speak for themselves, without the aid of this preface. But it may be interesting to know something of the circumstances of their composition. In 1985, more than six hundred men and women from more than seventy countries gathered in McAfee, New Jersey, to participate in an Assembly of World Religions.

They came from Buddhist, Christian, Confucian, Hindu, Jewish, Moslem, Sikh, Zoroastrian, primal African, and newer religious movements. The conference theme was "The Recovery of the Classical Heritage." During a week of prayer and meditation, dialogue groups, plenary addresses, cultural/ritual performances, and informal meetings, the participants struggled to find ways of meeting and sharing with one another across the differences of religion, race, and culture.

Perhaps one of the most important discoveries of that meeting was the awareness that one does not have to forsake one's deepest convictions or cultural traditions to discover and to value the special gifts of other traditions and ways. Rather, through plumbing the depths of their own respective faiths and cultures, the group became closer. At that level, they began to discover a "language of the heart" that speaks more profoundly than the "words" that often separate people. It is in this context that participants were invited to write these "letters to young people." The hope was that ways might be found to express to a new generation, one perhaps less scarred by the history of antagonism between religious traditions, the heritages that are carried in the lives and hearts of these epistles.

Given the circumstances under which these letters were written, it is not surprising that they exhibit a deep respect for faiths other than their own. Many of the letters mention the writers' "respect for others." It is worth noting that that respect does not diminish the authors' own commitments to their own traditions. Reflected here is not a lowest-common-denominator approach to religion, but a respect for the diverse gifts that have been given to us in the religious traditions of our common planet. The challenge is not to deny the faith of the other or to give up one's own, but, as one of the letters expressed it, "to find a way for people of different races, cultures, persuasions and convictions to live together peacefully."

This task confronts us all with increasing urgency. Not only do we all live in the shadow of nuclear and environmental catastrophe, but we are all also hurt by the continuing conflicts that arise in nations, between groups, within families, and in our own hearts because we have failed to find the ways that make for peace. If we can create bonds across generations—bonds of love, mutuality, and respect—then, perhaps, we can begin to discover ways to heal our divisions while rejoicing in our diversity. It is certainly the hope of the authors of these letters that they can contribute to such ends.

Thus we are pleased to commend these letters to your reading in the hope that they become gifts that will find their proper place in your lives and hearts.

November 11, 1988
Remembrance Day

Susan Hodges Bryant
M. Darrol Bryant

Letters to Young People

Dear Son,

When I look at you, so hopeful and yet so vulnerable, I feel I should at least let you know what I see.

You will soon be surrounded by all kinds of people vying for your attention and, even more, for your commitment. If it were only a question of selling you a product, I would not worry, for you would, sooner or later, find our yourself what suited you best. What worries me is that you are going to be encircled by all types of religions, all claiming to have the truth, to say the truth, to be the truth. And I am afraid you will fall into either a state of confusion that, in the long run, will make you despair of reaching any truth, or into the fanaticism of thinking you own the truth. Then the danger is twofold: that you may oppose all those who do not have "the truth" and that you may feel you do not need to look for it any longer.

What I wish for you is the humility to know that the search for truth is endless and, although it sometimes is a very lonely task, it is always done *for* others, not against them, because it is done *for*, not against, yourself.

Religion is a word you will hear a lot, but it is a reality you will seldom, if ever, find. Most people who will approach you as *religious* or *religion-bearing* either will not know what they are talking about or will want to exploit your naiveté and your desire for truth.

The reason that I have not talked to you about *religion* is that I wanted you to be a *real* man, so that you would be able to find a *real* religion. He who is not real, who is not himself to start with, will live in an imaginary world, will be a fictitious person, and therefore will be easy prey to all kinds of illusions and deceivers. I always insisted that you be yourself, that you find your own truth, because that is the only way you can sincerely say you love the truth; you found it and you strove for it. You can be fooled and fool yourself for the rest of your life if you cling to a truth that is only verbal or emotional or authoritarian. But you certainly cannot be mistaken if you endeavor to be your own real and truthful self.

I know this process is not easy. You will be tempted to look for the easy consolation of a ready-made truth, whether it becomes you or not. Even more, you will be pressed and perhaps goaded to follow the majority, who are happy with their illusions and will fight until the death not to have them taken away. But then what would be the meaning of your life? Why should I have imparted you life, if it were only for you to be one more circus spectator?

If, on the contrary, you learn to be true, to be as transparent as possible (as I try to be to you, and I do not advocate an imitation of me, but the development of your own integrity), then you will be ready to recognize any truth and any authentic person, wherever they may appear. Your utter sincerity in *being* will enable you to appreciate any real truth and to abhor any fiction or lie, even if it looks beautiful, useful, or profitable.

Ever since you were small, I worried about your becoming a victim of drug peddlers. Then I learned that if I taught you to care for reality, you would not care for a world of fantasy. Today I reiterate: I want you to be so faithful to your own reality, to your own truth, to your own unequivocal being, that you will be immunized against any temptation to lose yourself in the realm of a chemical or mental fantasy.

No, I do not want you to be like me; I want you to be like you. For that is the only way you will find the truth as far as it is available to you: not in others, not in books, not in rites or myths, but in yourself. I am not saying that all these things and people cannot help you. But if you ever felt they were trying to make you believe that you should forego your truth for theirs, you should be strong enough to turn them down, just as the man who lives fully in reality turns down drug dealers.

My son, I recognize that it would be much easier for me and

for you if I just said to you, "This is the truth; follow it." Or if I said, "God wants you to be so and so and to do this and that." But I do not want you to fall into the same trap I fell into so often—the trap of *not being*, in exchange for being comforted and feeling important.

There will be days when you might even hate me for requiring so much from you, for requiring that you be real and true, instead of letting you slip into the slumber of an easy belief. But most of the time I am sure you will love me, because if it is hard to be a real man, it would be much harder, in the long run, not to be anybody . . .

Because I love you I want you to be who you truly are. And the only real reason I would deserve your love is not that I gave you biological life (any animal can do that), but that, as far as I could, I made it possible for you to become a real, true, religious man.

Your father,

Emir Calluf
Curitiba, Brazil

Dear Youth,

I sometimes wish that each one of us had been given two lives within this present life—one life to learn how to live, and the other life to actually live. When we look back on our lives, we find that they are full of many mistakes and blunders; we find that we have been slow to learn. Sometimes we realize that it has taken us years to learn one lesson, a lesson that could have saved us many tears and much sadness and confusion. Since it is impossible to have those two lives on this earth, the best we can do is to pass on to the next generation the lessons that life has taught us, so that our children can benefit from our personal experience.

As I review my life, certain lessons stand out clearly. Some of my realizations reveal that the universe is run by law, not by chance; to be happy in this life and in the life to come, man must put God first in everything; anyone who wishes to be successful in life must have a vision; man must realize that people are more important than things.

One should always keep in mind that the whole universe is run by law and not by chance. Life is not casual but causal. The present condition of humanity is largely the result of our obedience or disobedience to the laws of the universe. As one writer has put it, "All our enjoyment or suffering may be traced back to obedience or transgression of natural laws." When Paul says in Galations 6:7, "Be not deceived; God is not mocked; for whatsoever a man soweth, that shall he also reap," he is telling us in another way that life operates according to law. Pharoah drowned the baby boys born to the Israelites, but he was also drowned in the Red Sea with his army. Jacob deceived his father about his favorite son, but he was also deceived about his favorite son by his boys. As surely as night follows day, so surely is cause followed by effect.

To be happy in this life and in the life to come, one must put God first in his thinking. The Bible begins with God, "In the beginning God . . ." (Gen. 1:1).

The ten commandments begin thus: "I am the Lord thy God . . ." (Ex. 20:2). The Lord's Prayer begins with, "Our Father . . ." What God is telling us in all of this is that our relationship with Him comes before anthing else. Worship is a relationship with God, and that relationship should take priority over everything else. The greatest mistake we have made and still are making is that we put things first and then if there is a little time left over, we give it to God.

The Bible states very emphatically, "Where there is no vision, the people perish" (Prov. 29:18). Visions are important and very necessary. They serve us as guides to our lives and our activities. They serve us as the north star, showing us our positions in the progress of life.

It is a sad thing to see a young person who has no vision, or one who has lost his life's vision. To such a person, life has no meaning whatsoever. Actually, such a person is not living, but simply existing. Such a person is a danger to or a burden on society. That is the reason the Bible says, "Where there is no vision, the people perish." Therefore, have a vision of the omnipotent God, who is the source of all true knowledge, wisdom, and power. Have a vision of all the potentialities that God has put in you, and under his guidance, devise ways and means whereby you can actualize those potentialities. Look at the world's needs and at those who are less fortunate than you are, and then envision what they can become when Christian young men and women put their resources together and say *barambie* for a better world.

The Bible tells us of a young man who had seen the Lord in a vision. As he beheld the glory and majesty of Almighty God, his immediate reaction was, "Woe is me, for I am undone because

I am a man of unclean lips, and I dwell in the midst of a people of unclean lips, for mine eyes have seen the King, the Lord of hosts." As the panorama progresses, the young man is transformed. The live coal from the altar of God touches his unclean lips, and they become clean, his iniquity is taken away, and his sin is purged.

Then he was able to hear the voice of God asking, "Whom shall I send?" The young man's answer was immediate and definite: "Here am I; send me" (Isa. 6:1–8). This is what happens when a young person sees a vision of God, of himself, and of humanity and its needs.

Lastly, I would like to submit that people are infinitely more important than things. When we read the ten commandments given by the Lord on Mount Sinai, we can see that people are more important than things. When we read the commandments in the order they are given, which is an order of importance, the first concern is God; the second is people; and the last is things. ("Thou shalt not covet anything that is thy neighbour's.")

Why was the rich man in Luke 12:20 called a "fool"? As far as we human beings are concerned, he was not a fool; he was a hard-working man. There is nothing wrong in working hard and becoming rich; it is commendable. Then, we ask, why did the Lord call him "thou fool"? The simple answer is that man had his priorities all mixed up. To him things were first, and God, the giver of all good gifts, was forgotten. Man had no time for the poor and the needy. All we read in the story is "my fruits, my barns, my goods," etc. But things, as important as they may be, do not love. They do not go to heaven. And they cannot take us to heaven. People are more important than things because they are created in the image of God. They have feelings; they are candidates for the kingdom of God. Therefore, stop and take stock and ask: Where do I spend most of my time? How much do I spend on things? How much on people? How much on God?

Let me conclude with a text found in Matthew 6:33: "But seek ye first the kingdom of God and his righteousness, and all these things shall be added unto you."

Sincerely,

Truneh Wolde Selassie
Seventh-Day Adventist, Ethiopia

Dear Jaswant Singh Sat Siri Akal,

I was happy to learn from your letter that you have settled down and have taken up your studies seriously. Your future will depend a good deal on your present efforts to build up a worthwhile career. A good education and professional qualifications are a sure passport to success in this age of expertise and excellence. But knowledge and skill without a life of righteousness fail to bring happiness in spite of an abundance of material comforts and social contacts.

In Sikhism human perfection—physical, moral, and spiritual—is the goal, and it can be achieved by the practice of certain religious and moral truths. Religion alone is the source of moral insight and ethical action for the individual. In our faith the spiritual path involves a minimum of ritual. Sikh meditation does not necessitate special postures or physical gestures. You can, for example, recite the morning prayer or *Japji* while getting ready for the day. An intellectual perception of truth, however, is not enough. Worship without good deeds has no meaning. "Of all religions," says Guru Arjan, "the highest is to meditate on the Name of God and perform noble deeds." Personal social service is highly regarded in Sikhism. "A place in God's court can only be attained if we do service to others in the world," said Guru Nanak. Sikhism is not a hermetically sealed "spiritual affair" but a religion that emphasizes both the dimension of prayer and worship and the dimension of selfless service to humanity.

We live in a society with a plurality of faiths. Religions which make for division and discord play into the hands of the opponents of religion. Sikhs have never claimed that their religion is the best or the only way to approach God. The Sikh gurus stood for harmony and concord. "They who are united with

God are the friends of all men," said Guru Arjan. Sikhs in no way, therefore, give offence to other faiths. The gurus emphasized human equality and the ultimate oneness of mankind. "All creatures in the world are born of the same spirit," said Guru Nanak. Fanaticism and bigotry are thus alien to our tradition. The Sikh is called to see God's light shining in others, whatever their religious persuasion.

Permissiveness is an evil prevalent in our society today. Since Sikhs are known for their moral discipline, any laxity in your conduct could reflect negatively on our religious tradition. Guru Gobind Singh's words, "It is the ethical living of a Sikh that is dear to me and not his being a Sikh," should be your motto.

Yours
affectionately,

Piara Singh Sambhi
Leeds, England

My dear Children

Why remain Jewish, you may ask me? In this secular and often brutal world we can, indeed, ask "why?" Why, after the attempted destruction of our people during World War II, and the continued travail of our reestablished homeland, Israel, should we choose to remain Jewish? Have our people not paid too large a price? Perhaps, above all, because of these factors we should be determined to retain our heritage. But this is a negative reason. What is there of abiding value in our faith that demands its survival, a survival that can only be assured by us ourselves?

All faiths have a strong ethical content, and all religions have distinctive rituals. All spiritual traditions are of infinite value. Thus our faith is of infinite value to us. Its ethics, rituals, and rich traditions provide us with ways to relate to God, his creation, our fellow human beings, and nature.

We, like seekers in other traditions, encounter certain apparent ambiguities and paradoxes in the holy scriptures. Of these, one of the most misunderstood of all our doctrines is that of chosenness. We are taught that God chose us from among all the nations of the world as his special treasure, a people who were destined to stand alone and not be like other nations. What is most often misunderstood is that this is by no means a suggestion of racial superiority. We were chosen to enter into a covenant with God, and that covenant brings special obligations that cover every aspect of life.

The Torah instructs us how to live and, therefore, governs our behavior. The Torah sealed the covenant which God entered into with us when He delivered us from bondage in Egypt and led us to the land He promised us, *Eretz Yisrael*. The Torah has been interpreted over centuries by the rabbis in the Talmud. Through the Talmud we were taught to walk through this life in such a way that we sanctify the everyday act. In each small action we are to remain cognizant of God the creator, and be reminded that we, as the peak of God's creation, are responsible stewards over this creation. As the crown of creation, we may be tempted to laud ourselves, but if we remain true to God's intention for us, thereby remaining in the right relationship with God and man, we will be able to journey through life with dignity and respect for all living things.

We are the first people within the biblical tradition to whom monotheism was revealed. In a sense, therefore, we gave monotheism to the world. According to Christians, centuries after the Exodus, God revealed Himself again through Jesus of Nazareth, thereby making his divine grace available to a far larger sector of humanity. In the seventh century C.E., the prophet Muhammad brought to the world what Muslims regard as the last and definitive revelation of God to mankind. As Jews, however, we hold firm to our belief that God will redeem the world by sending his Messiah at the end of days.

Our relationship with these other faiths has never been easy because our basic claims are so different. Our doctrine of chosenness seems, somehow, to be a scandal which the world finds difficult to reconcile with God's universality. Because of this doctrine, we have suffered much. We ourselves do not grasp the full import of it. It is the greatest mystery of Jewish existence. As a "light unto the nations" were we, perhaps, destined for special suffering? In the year 70 C.E., our temple and holy city, Jerusalem, were destroyed and, thereafter, our people were scattered. Bereft of a homeland for two thousand years, we were forced to adapt our religious tradition to a situation of powerlessness. Nonetheless, we have survived as a people.

Our daily actions and our yearly round of festivals and sabbaths, commanded in our Torah, have kept the Jewish people alive. They have given us an oasis in the midst of the dispersion and degradation that have characterized so much of our history. In 1948 the land of Israel was reestablished as our national and spiritual homeland. This event ended our powerlessness and our vulnerability. For this reason we need to ensure that Israel is maintained.

As you grow to adulthood, you will remember well the festivals that we have celebrated yearly since you were babies. You still treasure the family togetherness that arises out of our sitting down together to commemorate the Exodus at Passover or *Pesach*, taking delight in the real experience of freedom. You still revel in the luxuriant, cool fragrance of the *Succah*, which we build and decorate each year to commemorate God's protection of us when we were wandering in the wilderness on our way to the Promised Land. You still approach the Days of Awe with hope and creaturely fear and contingency. At the same time, as each of these events rolls around, you remember with sadness the close friends and relatives who were here with us in years past, and now are deceased. These rituals mark their value and their passing.

Retain the observance of the festivals and teach your children of the beauty and family-centeredness of Judaism. Give them the best possible chance to acquire a Jewish education, for Judaism, in addition to being believed in, has to be lived, and your children can only imbibe its essence through emulation and education. Focus your attention on the well-being of Israel, for as long as we have Israel, we cannot be a powerless people again. Bear in mind that powerlessness led us to suffer the Holocaust!

In this world of secularization and strife, remember that Judaism, the religion into which we were born, is our surest way of relating to God. This is our only way of elevating ourselves to truly human status. It might not be better than any other way, but it has a proud history indeed and it is ours alone. Its beauty touches our very souls, reminding us that as children of

God, we can, as his co-workers, work with all creation to ensure a better future and a better world for all the generations to come.

With affection,

Jocelyn Helleq
Johannesburg, South Africa

My dear Amitabh,

Thank you very much for your affectionate letter. I am delighted to know that you are in search of an authentic existence. It gives me great pleasure to know that at this young age you are contemplating philosophical questions like the meaning of existence. Your letter has sparked me to reflect on the goal and purpose of human life. Philosophers of different age and cultures have also tried to define the nature of man and society. After studying many different philosophies and *isms*, however, I feel that Buddhism alone can lead a man from the dualism of subject-object, material-ideal, agnostic-gnostic, science-religion, to an authentic, nondualistic human existence.

Furthermore, the Buddhist concepts of Nirvana and nonviolence are more relevant today even than they were at the time of Lord Buddha. Today the alternative to the philosophy of nonviolence and Nirvana is destruction of the earth. I am writing this letter to you to make you aware of the hollowness of our technological culture, the danger of our consumer society, and the threat of nuclear holocaust. I hope you will give serious thought to my letter and if you find any merit therein, please discuss it with your friends.

With my love and affection,
Yours in the Dharma,

Wilbagedara Dhammika
Bodhgaya, India

My dear Divakar,

I am writing this letter to you on a subject which I have often discussed with you. I firmly believe that our Hindu religious tradition is one of the greatest spiritual traditions of the world. I have had the good fortune of not only being born into it, but also of studying and imbibing it to the best of my ability. I deeply feel the necessity of letting you know what appear to be the most important resources from this tradition so that you can keep the torch burning.

As you know, the most important written transmitters of our spiritual tradition are the Vedas, the Upanishads, the Ramayana, and the Bhagavad-gita. The most ancient as well as the most important of the Vedas is the Rigveda. The most celebrated Upanishad is the Brhadaranyaka Upanishad. Each of these four great books contains gems of wisdom illustrative of the central legacy I would like to pass on to you.

First, I have selected two passages from the Rigveda. The first passage says, "There is one Eternal Being whom the wise men call by many names." By saying that wise men call God by many names, the Rigveda indirectly recognizes that all religions worshipping the same God by different names are really different paths to the same goal. The second passage is the famous Gayatri prayer which says, "Let us meditate on the excellent glory of God, the vivifier, that He may inspire your thoughts." This passage shows that according to our spiritual tradition, the most precious gift of God to human beings is their power of thinking, by which they can discriminate between right and wrong as well as create and invent various useful things.

The Brhadaranyaka Upanishad contains a beautiful parable according to which the Creator imparted knowledge to his three sons—an angel, a man, and a demon. He uttered the letter c to each of them as his final piece of advice and asked each one to explain what he understood it to mean. The first son, who lived in the luxury of heaven, interpreted it as control of the senses; the second son, who earned bread only for himself and his family, interpreted it as charity; and the third son, who was temperamentally cruel, interpreted it as clemency. Through the medium of this parable, the Upanishad has emphasized three cardinal virtues: self-control, charity, and kindness. Likewise, another passage of the same Upanishad narrates an event of great cultural and spiritual significance. When the great rishi Vajnavalkya claimed the prize announced by King Janaka of Videha for the best scholar of theology, the most noted among the scholars who challenged him was a learned lady named Gargi Vachanknavi, who had been invited by the king to his court along with other famous scholars. This incident shows that women held an honored place in society in Vedic times.

The Ramayana portrays the ideal life of Lord Rama, who willingly went into exile to keep the word of his father, showered love on his brothers, set the ideal of monogamy by marrying only one wife, and greeted the most lowly as well as the most exalted persons with the same warmth and affection. Thus adherence to truth, support of family concord, and avoidance of discrimination among persons on grounds of birth and position are the key notes of the Ramayana.

The Bhagavad-gita is an elegant poem containing the noble sermon of Lord Krishna to Arjuna. The central teaching of this great book is that a person should devotedly perform his duty without being concerned about or obsessed with its reward.

To sum up, belief in the oneness of God; the cultivation of good thoughts; the practice of the virtues of self-control, charity, and kindness; the accordance of an honored place to women in society; the adherence to truth, family concord, and equality of all human beings; and the performance of one's duty without any thought of its reward constitute the central legacy of Hinduism which I wish to pass on to you to practice and to propagate.

With love and best wishes,
Your affectionate father,

Purushottam L. Bhargava
Jaipur, India and
Hamilton, Ontario, Canada

Dear Young Friends,

This letter is timely, for the leaders of the nations of the world shall soon be gathering at the United Nations to reassert their pledge "to save future generations from the scourge of war . . . and to reaffirm faith in fundamental human rights, in the dignity and worth of human persons, in the equal rights of men and women and of nations large and small, and to establish conditions under which justice and respect for the weak and obligations to fellow men . . . can be maintained, and to promote social progress and better standards of life in larger freedom."

In a world afflicted with strife, misery, poverty, hunger, antagonism, distrust, fear, uncertainty, and despair, these promises may seem to be illusory, but continued allegiance to them and promotion of them is extremely important. People of vision and good will look upon you, the youth of the world, to carry the torch and finish humankind's uncompleted task.

As custodians of the human legacy and as carriers of human civilization, standing at the brink of despair and hope, you are the key to human survival. Your responsibilities are, therefore, immense. But once you take up the banner of peace, justice, equity, amity, and unity, all forces of war, injustice, inequity, enmity, and disunity shall be crushed.

Faith in the sanctity of life and belief in the dignity of human persons are central to this resolve, from which shall flow the strength to proclaim and protect the rights not only of yourself, but also of others. Your obligations are many, i.e., unto yourself, your fellow human beings, society as a whole, your fellow creatures, the cosmos, and above all, to the Creator, the Lord of the Universe. Although you must care for yourself, you must also care for and protect the rights of others.

An individual must be regarded as a pearl, strung on a thread of human fraternity, living in unison with fellow creatures. Such a physically, intellectually, psychologically, aesthetically, morally, and spiritually united society will be in harmony with the endowments of the earth and of the universe and will be in consonance with the ultimate reality of the Oneness of the Divine.

Only in the preservation and advancement of such a wholesome tradition can a purposeful life be imagined. In putting trust in you, I believe that you will not falter, but will succeed in ushering in a better tomorrow, without discrimination, for us all.

Yours,

Dr. Inamullah Khan
Secretary General
Motamar Al - Alam Al - Islami
(World Muslim Congress)
Karachi, Pakistan

Dear Young Friend,

You have been born into a very exciting world during a period of both intense darkness and intense light. Many find the dark side overwhelming and therefore are afraid that we will end up in a total catastrophe in the near future. Every day the media bring news of disasters, crimes, and destructive activities from everywhere. We are so beseiged with bad news that we hardly react anymore. In spite of this bad news, however, a lot of people, old and young, all over the world, concentrate on watching the signals of light—and take postive, unifying, non-violent, and constructive initiatives and actions! They trust in their different ways that the Great One (or Ones) to whom they have given a holy name is still "holding the whole world in his hands" and will not allow dark powers to pass beyond certain limits.

A great number of young people are willingly and enthusiastically giving their time, strength, and devotion to ideals and movements where they recognize these signals of light—both in traditional and New Age organizations. Others go as individuals to alleviate suffering, start groups for peace, and support others in building a better future. All around us we can see the war being waged between darkness and light. Wars, conflicts, dangerous experiments, greed, and selfishness are rampant. And yet at the same time there is so much concern for the well-being of others, so many good activities.

No one can calculate the balance between the darkness and the light. It is obviously most important which side we are on; I mean you and I! It is no longer only a private business of feeling satisfaction and meaning in our own lives; we must realize that by our choice we are adding a weight on one of the sides.

You may be acquainted with stories and legends of both the

East and the West about great heroes and their fights against enemies of all kinds. The real legends can all be read in a symbolic way, experienced at a level of deeper meaning. A rather well-known group of such stories are the Grail legends of King Arthur and his knights of the Round Table. A number of books have been translated into many languages on the topic of the quest for the Holy Grail. In these stories knights fight against green dragons, save noble ladies from castle prisons, kill cruel rulers, and protect the weak and poor. If we read these tales at a deeper level, we recognize ourselves and our fellow human beings, fighting against the "green dragon" of selfishness, greed, and envy, trying to release the "inner beauty" of the divine spark inside ourselves in order to let our light shine where it is needed.

These legends about the adventures of the great quest of all seekers also contain the story of your own inner journey. They speak to the questions " 'Why was I born?' 'What is the purpose of my life?' 'Where do I come from and where do I—and my dear ones—go after death?' "

The Knights of the Round Table found out that by fulfilling their quest and nourishing their own flame, they added to the light in the world in a time of darkness. And so did the heroes of all real legends . . . I would like to tell you—if you don't know it already—that there is a youth movement called the International Round Table for young people that was created to serve the light in our own time. It is now active in twenty-four countries in groups called Tables and its members are of different races, religions, creeds, etc. Members are admitted to the Order by becoming pages, and later on they advance to the rank of companion, squire, and knight.

The members of the Round Table meet to perform simple, beautiful ceremonies that remind them they are flames of God, as are their brothers and sisters. The life motto of the members of the International Round Table is "Live pure, speak true, right wrong, follow the King." (The word *king* symbolizes the highest ordering principle in human society. It has many other names in the various world traditions.) The Round Table also coordinates a variety of activities for members: nature excursions, handicrafts, theatrical productions, animal studies, and camping—nationally and internationally, and social outreach—to the aged, the handicapped, and children in need.

Each year the Senior Knight, the International Head of the Order, announces a theme for the year. In 1986, for example, the theme was "Try to understand and make friends with those you meet whom you do not like or agree with!" The aim of this theme is to build bridges between people who otherwise would remain unconnected.

To those of us who work for it, the International Order of the Round Table is one of the hopeful signs of our time. Should you feel this way too and be interested in knowing more about this work, you are welcome to write to me or to the Chief Secretary (address below).

Remember, wherever you go and whomever you meet, you have the power to either reduce or increase the light in our world by the way you choose to live your life—even in the smallest detail!

    Yours,

    Ingrid Nyborg-Fjellander
    Lidingo, Sweden
    Chief Secretary of The International Round Table:
    Mrs. Philippa Hartley,
    11 Woodland Ave.
    Coventry CV56DD, England

Dear Young Brother,

I speak to you as a highly educated man in Western culture and at the same time as an African deeply rooted in the values of Black civilization. I am adept in the voodoo religion ennobled by Christianity. What are the most important resources from my spiritual tradition that become its central legacy? A legacy that I wish to pass on to you? It is the love and peace that proceed from a life lived according to the spirit of God. As a practitioner of an African traditional religion ennobled, as I said, by Christianity, I am not advocating syncretism. I would, however, refer you to St. Paul's words to the Hebrews: "In the past God spoke to our forefathers through the prophets at many times and invarious ways, but in these last days he has spoken to us by his son, whom he appointed heir of all things and through whom he made the universe."

God has always spoken through our various world traditions. In recognition of this truth, Pope Paul VI received, in 1975 in Rome, for the first time in the history of the Church, a delegation of voodoo priests from Togo. And then in August of 1985, Pope John Paul II prayed together with voodoo priests near their temple at Togoville in Togo.

Voodoo is not a religion of fear. If there is any fear at all, it is that of being alienated from God, of being insufficiently protected by his spirit. To be united to God is to be full of the love of justice and tolerance. African oral traditions and history ignore religious wars and sectarianism. African religion is a cosmic liturgy; it is a humanization of nature and a spiritualization of man.

The world, you see, dear young brother, can be destroyed today because man is afraid of man. We can avoid destruction by becoming closer to God. A number of ancient authors, like

Homera and Diodorus Sicilicus, wrote that the African is the most religious man on earth. Let us, therefore, fill ourselves with the spirit of God today more than ever so that peace may reign among all men and women of the world.

Yours,

Anonymous
Lome, Togo, West Africa

Dear Young Friend,

I believe that all positive religions have high ethical and moral values, but only one of them offers itself to you as an authentic possibility for your own life's journey. Christianity, Buddhism, Judaism, and Islam, for example, set universal standards of behavior that link humankind to the transcendental. All these paths are on the same ethical scale, but only one of them can be your specific pathway; only one can provide you with the religious attitude that will give you full effectiveness and security.

It is true that because of the threat of imminent death that faces mankind, everything has colluded to disturb what Kant called "the secure passage through life" or *Der sichere Gang*. It is therefore more urgent than ever to create new perspectives. My religion and my scientific research have convinced me that technical advances have led contemporary man to a unilateralism that prevents him from perceiving what lies beyond those advances. Our impressive material advances have brought not happiness or triumph, but fear, confusion, uncertainty, anxiety, and sadness.

In order to overcome the evils in our world, you need to understand that you are neither the beginning nor the end, that you are not your own root nor the master of history. This means that the solution to our predicament lies in going beyond subjectivity and changing our attitude towards life, taking it as a gift for which we need to be accountable.

In a Zen Buddhist legend a young man asked his master, "What should I do to teach enlightenment?" And the master gave the same reply three times: "Be watchful!"

Christianity, in turn, tells us to love our neighbour, God, and nature. Through being watchful and experiencing love, we can find the peace and harmony that will enable us to recover "the secure passage through life."

With affection,

Miriama Widakowich Weyland

Greetings, my Brother,

I greet you in the spirit of our heritage, forged by our ancestors throughout the centuries, a spirit of brotherhood, even with those whom we have not known but to whom we were doubtless united by blood relationship or by friendship.

Perhaps you know the fable of the laborer. He promised his sons he would give them a treasure without price as an inheritance—a treasure he had prepared for them. Days passed . . . then months . . . then years. Finally, when the father was near death, the sons came together to ask him for this famous treasure. Then the old man revealed that the promised treasure was nothing other than the earth—that which he had cultivated and from which he had been able to live and prosper.

In reality the earth is a treasure not because it is earth, but because it is the conveyor of life. It is thus life that is the supreme treasure. The wisdom of nations, and most particularly of our ancestors, understood this well. The best wishes that could be extended to a young man and his bride were to have many children, for children are a blessing from God, from whom we all come.

Life is such a treasure that it must be tended with care and helped to grow. If a cook does not perform his duties well, he will be dismissed. He knows that in such a case he will be rejected and will have no choice but to disappear, because he has become an obstacle to life and to the growth of the community.

Without doubt you've had the opportunity to participate in the funerals of elderly people. On these occasions, rather than shedding tears, one celebrates life with songs and dances. And it further honors life when relatives put into the tomb with their loved one familiar objects such as sandals, a hat, perhaps even a pitcher and something to drink.

Without the gift of life, men could do nothing on this earth, and man's destruction would mark the end of all progress, not only for the individual, but for society as well. For those who have been educated in a world of traditional values, it is unthinkable that men could be killed because they were perceived as obstacles to a country's growth and expansion. The force and passion that kill, the revolutions that lead men to assassinate each other, bring about their own demise, whether in the short run or the long run, for nothing can take the place of life.

One thing has particularly struck me. It is that in all religions, the Divine, the Supreme Being, is always presented as the source of life, because it is the Divine that gives life and takes it away. The Bible, the Koran, the religious books of the East, the African traditions, all are in accord on this point.

Isn't there enough here to reflect on? How can we envision the advancement of man and of society without the advancement of life in all its dimensions? My brother, take note that the value of life surpasses all other wealth. Take up your life with an attitude of magnanimity, and help others to do the same.

Sincerely,

Anonymous

Dear Ravindra,

As you are aware, I am going shortly to America to participate in the Assembly of World Religions. "Can there be a world religion?" you may ask. Of course there cannot be only one religion that contains or subsumes all others. Although religious traditions are practiced by groups of people, religion is a matter for each individual, and one must make a faith commitment according to his or her own aptitude, understanding, and stage of development. Of course one of the predispositions that orients one to a specific religious tradition is being born into a particular family in particular circumstances.

In your case, for example, you were born into a family of Jains. Your family has followed certain Jain traditions which you have absorbed unconsciously. Now I would like to see you adopt and follow these traditions consciously, and with understanding. What are these traditions that you have been following and which you, too, will later pass on to your own children? These basic traditions include the following dicta:

1. Do not consciously kill or support the killing of any living being (even a small insect) capable of movement.

2. Recite *Navkar-mantra* while getting up in the morning and when going to bed at night. Recite this mantra whenever you are in difficulty.

3. Visit your religious head often. Keep in touch with monks and nuns of your tradition.

4. Observe a full-day fast (for twenty-four hours) on *Samvatsari* day (a Jain festival, you know). Recall your deeds of the past year on that day.

5. Forgive others and ask for forgiveness for all the mistakes you have made against them. Do this on the next day of the fast.

6. Never uproot a tree of a size equal to or greater than your arm's width.

7. Give up eating at least one foodstuff—to be named, just as I have left *branzyl* for life.

I pray that you will listen to this advice of mine.

Yours,

M. C. Bhandari
Calcutta, India

My beloved Sons! My darling Daughters!

Let the future of the world be pure, with your hearts beating in unison.
Let your thoughts be pure like the glistening rare pearls under the deep waters of the ocean.
Let your hearts rise like the Himalayan peaks and pray for universal peace and a trouble-free life.
Be aware that you carry the responsibility to strive for the welfare of the world by reducing your own selfish needs.
Let your minds overflow with noble ideals, right principles, and compassion towards all life.
Develop the patience of the earth, the strength of the mountain, the prosperity of the ocean, and the purity of the sky.
May God protect you from becoming victims of evil habits.
Be alert, active, and busy like the bee.
Have an open mind, enjoy the company of the good, and lead a disciplined life.
May you prosper and progress in every way.
May God bless you with beauty, health, knowledge, and wisdom.
Let there be peace everywhere.

Om Shanti! Shanti! Shanti!

Her Holiness Dr. Sayi Matha Siva Brinda Devi
Pudukkottai, South India

My dear son Kenedy,

I wish that I could leave you with much wealth when it comes time for me to die. However, I am not a millionaire and there is no prospect of my becoming one. More important than material wealth, though, is a spiritual inheritance. Thus I would like to bequeath to you the spiritual legacy I received from my father, your grandfather. Hear now, my son, pearls of wisdom from our Christian tradition, from the holy scriptures:

"Every word of God is pure; he is a shield to them that put their trust in him." "The rich and the poor meet together in the Lord, for he is the maker of them all." "Train up a child in the way he should go, and when he is old, he will not depart from it." "Commit your works to the Lord and your thoughts shall be established . . . When a man's ways please the Lord, he makes his enemies to be at peace with him . . ." "Pride goes before destruction and a haughty spirit before a fall." "He that is slow to anger is better than the mighty, and he that rules his spirit than he that takes a city . . ." "The fear of the Lord is the beginning of wisdom . . ." "He that walks with wise men shall be wise, but a companion of fools shall be destroyed."

My son Kenedy, hear the instruction I give you, and do not forsake the counsel of your mother. Do not let mercy and truth forsake you; bind them around your neck; write them on the walls of your heart. Thus you shall find favor and understanding in the sight of God and man.

The Bible says, "Trust in the Lord with all your heart and do not lean on your own understanding. In all your ways acknowledge the Lord and he will direct your paths. Fear the Lord and depart from evil."

My son, do not forsake the advice of your parents. The commandments of the Lord shall be a lamp unto your feet and a light unto your pathway. Remember that he who causes the righteous to go astray shall himself fall into his own pit.

The Word of God tells us, "Open rebuke is better than secret love. Faithful are the wounds of a friend, but the kisses of an enemy are deceitful. Withdraw your feet from your neighbor's house lest he grow weary of you and so hate you." "A man who bears a false witness against his neighbour is a sword and a sharp arrow." "Confidence in an unfaithful man in time of trouble is like a broken tooth, and a foot out of joint." "If your enemy is hungry, give him food to eat and if he is thirsty, give him water to drink."

Hear, my son, be wise and live according to the way of the Lord. Do not linger among winebibbers and those who live riotously. Do not despise your parents when they grow old. Buy the truth and sell it not.

Your father,

M. J. Chidzungu
Kasungu, Malawi

My dear Young People,

One of the greatest evils of our time has been the rapidly spreading forces of disintegration at almost all levels of society. Competition, conflict, greed, and the demise of moral values have become the order of the day. The world appears to be heading straight for a crisis in interpersonal, interreligious, and international relationships.

If the forces of disunity are to be countered, our heritages—whatever their denomination—must be revived. Every religion is basically committed to the values of unity, peace, and spirituality. These values are the only force that can prevail against the future crisis.

I am a Hindu by birth and by practice. What my religion teaches me is the virtue of understanding and tolerance vis-à-vis different faiths, viewpoints, opinions, and beliefs. The leaders of my tradition have always insisted on one's being open to the worldviews of others. I would like to tell you, in the light of my own personal experience, that to understand others is to get into their inner selves, to realize that it is possible to see the world as others are seeing it. I would advise you to cultivate within you the sense that all of us are ultimately the products of the same designer—God—and therefore to be in peace and harmony is to be *in* Him.

With my cordial wishes,

Mrs. N. R. Sinari

Beloved Youth:

Although most adults do not set a good example for the youth of today, what I would most wish for you is an attitude that cultivates love, peace, work, awareness, responsibility, spontaneity, and play. Thus I pray that adults today learn to *live* and to *be* those things they preach. Then perhaps they will be able to set a good example for youth. I know that you already possess, in your youthful nature, many of the virtues we grown-ups want to teach you.

So, let us, hand in hand, walk the pathway towards the realization of these virtues in our lives. And above all, let me emphasize that once a day, and especially when in doubt, take time to listen! For a few moments forget all the words and all the *do's* and *don't's* you have ever learned—and listen to your body, your heart, and your soul. Listening is the key that will open the door of self-knowledge. And after a while you will come to know that your self is not separate from your friends' selves, your parents' selves, my self, and the seas' and the stars' selves.

After having listened intently to your inner knowledge, you will discover who you really are: a true Mr. Universe, a true Miss Universe!

Sincerely,

Nevzat Erkmen
Istanbul, Turkey

My dear Daughter Sawsan,

Next January you shall be sixteen years old. How fast time is going! You are a young woman and we must no longer treat you as a child. Your age is a critical one. It is called by Western societies "the age of consent." Within the Sudanese Muslim community, you are unlikely to have heard this phrase. It means that a girl is now legally entitled to give her consent to have sexual intercourse with the man she chooses. Thus the act is legal, irrespective of her marital relationship with the man involved.

In Islam the age of the girl is not the only criterion for the legality of the sexual act. In Islamic ethics the sexual act is only legitimate if it takes place between a married couple who have reached the age of puberty. The Holy Quran says, "And go not near *Zina* (fornication or adultery); surely it is an obscenity, and evil as a way" (17, 32). That statement does not mean Islam sees anything wrong with sex. On the contrary, in its legitimate form sex becomes a form of worshipping God, since it is done within the boundaries He defines.

You may well ask why Islam does not allow or condone an enjoyable act like sex outside the marital institution, especially if young men and women must wait for a number of years before they can get married. Let me just point out a general principle about Islamic ethics. All prohibitions in Islam are created for the general welfare of all human beings; that is, they are based on utilitarian grounds.

Islam perceives the family as the best basic unit of human society, a unit in which children are brought up and socialized. It is obvious that allowing sex, which is one of the strongest human desires, to be practiced outside the marital institution weakens the bond of the family. If this strong human attachment is confined to husband and wife, it is bound to strengthen and enhance their mutual relationship. Observing contemporary societies, one may reach the conclusion that the weakness of the family is almost proportionate to the laxity of that society with regard to sex. Islam views sex as a constructive, functional act in discouraging young men from getting married at an early age. Understandably, they seek to "enjoy" themselves without bearing any responsibility!

The consequences of a free-sex society are obvious to everyone who chooses to see: broken homes, illegitimate children, unmarried mothers, prostitution, juvenile crime, venereal disease, etc. Therefore, my beloved daughter, I think our old Islamic maxim that sex is only a "family affair" is still right and useful.

Ever yours,

Your father, Al-Abdin
Khartoum, Sudan

Dear daughters Eleonora and Florencia,

I was educated as a Catholic, but as a result of studying Indian philosophy, I also enjoyed the benefit of coming into contact with values that were different from mine—and those of my people. This contact allowed me to enrich and enlarge my own religious tradition. The interior encounter I experienced among such diverse traditions and values as Christianity, Buddhism, and Hinduism produced a personal crisis within me—a crisis from which I emerged as a more tolerant, more complete, and more human person.

If my experience could help you, my beloved daughters, my life would be justified; it would have a real meaning. It is from my personal experience and not from my knowledge—which is very minimal indeed—of religions and their values that I want to leave you a small, simple message for the future.

First of all, *love* is the key to a fulfilling life: love yourselves; love others; love truth, goodness, and beauty; love nature—the trees, the flowers, the sky, the stars. If you feel love, then you will be able to be compassionate with yourselves and with others. Being compassionate, you will be tolerant and respectful. Being tolerant and respectful, you will be nonviolent. This attitude will elicit love, compassion, tolerance, and respect from others. Then you will feel a special happiness, together with a sense of peace and well-being.

But, you may ask me, how do I know what is good for others and how to love them if they belong to different cultures and civilizations, if they have ideas, creeds, values, different from mine? Is it possible to love people who are so different from me? Is it possible to be tolerant of beliefs and habits so different from mine? Is it possible in the world today, as things are, to maintain traditional principles of morality? And is it even possible to maintain a religious commitment today? Is there really a place for religion in our modern world?

You, and others of your generation, will undoubtedly ask these, and many other, questions. I must tell you that I am not able to answer everything with certainty, but I can remind you that there are some values common to all men and women. True goodness transcends any particular religious tradition; it is the essence of religion in its widest and deepest sense; it is a part of all human beings; it always has been and always will be—so long as there is life on this planet.

I know that you will find your path in an authentic way. Work hard and be hopeful.

With love,

Your mother, Carmen Dragonetti
Argentina

Dear Young People of the World,

Greetings from the heart! I've only a few sentiments to offer you here, and it is my wish that somehow they will inspire you, even in the slightest, to pursue life with an immensity of boundless, unconditional love and joy.

There have been many battles among human beings since the beginning of time. Why do people bother to fight? Ask yourselves this question, for I am quite sure that in your musings, you shall find that war is steeped in absurdity. Take this to heart. Try to make it a practice among yourselves to be patient, tolerant, and compassionate towards others. Be good and true to yourselves as well, for purity of heart and mind emanating from the self is the greatest gift one can offer mankind. Do not forget how each individual on our planet is both significant and insignificant simultaneously. This realization can place one properly between humility and pride. Remember to be not only a preacher of virtue, but a true practitioner as well!

Take time each day to truly see the world around you—feel the warmth of the sun, the coolness of rain, see the colors of the rainbow, near the brook, the birds, the children. See the wonders of life. Appreciate the opportunity you have been given by virtue of being alive. Life is, indeed, precious. Remember to share and not to chastise others, for there is no place for malignant thoughts or gestures.

Raise your voices to create the most beautiful song of life. Rejoice in your short time on this earth and strive towards reaching the ultimate light.

Blessings to you all,

Lelitto Arganando

Dear Young Friend,

The fate of the world of tomorrow depends entirely on how it will be fashioned by today's youth, who will become tomorrow's leaders. The youth of the present age are beset with two serious problems. While Western youth suffer from a sense of complete isolation and loneliness, born of a long history of independence from parental control or supervision, Eastern youth suffer from a lack of self-reliance, born of a long history of protectionist parental control. Both these positions are detrimental to the development of the individual, as well as to the development of society. It is the middle path between these two positions that is the most beneficial to both the individual and society.

This middle path encourages one to pursue a course of action that makes one fully alert to the needs of others. On the other hand, this path also gives one self-reliance and encourages the fullest development of one's own personality.

The fact that one is born into this world as a member of a social group makes it obligatory that he or she remain conscious, in all his or her actions, of this basic social identity. Buddhist teaching emphasizes this fact in the determination of an individual's norms for action, in the determination of what is good and bad, of what is moral and immoral.

A course of action is good if it is rooted in non-greed, non-ill-will, and non-delusion and produces results that are beneficial to both the initiator of the action and its recipient. One must always be conscious, not only of his own good, but also of the good of others. In other words, a high degree of social awareness is demanded at all levels of thinking and action.

As a member of a social group, one finds that one's duties and obligations towards the other group members determine what is good and proper or what is bad and improper. As a parent, one has parental duties and obligations towards his children; the children in turn have their own duties and obligations towards their parents. Duties and obligations are also inherent in being a teacher, a pupil; a wife, a husband; an employer, an employee; a priest, a layperson.

When one's duties and obligations are determined by these reciprocal relationships, not only is it not possible to become too self-centered and egotistic in one's aspirations or actions; it is also not possible to be isolated and left out of society, as there are reciprocal needs that demand attention. These duties do not, however, hinder in any way the development of one's personality, for one is free to develop to the highest possible level.

As a member of today's younger generation, not only must you view yourself in terms of your relationship to the other members of your society; you must also be alert to the demands that such membership makes obligatory. It is important that you realize that it is only by fulfilling these obligations that you become a full member of society.

With all best wishes,

Dr. M.M.J. Marasinghe
Theravada Buddhist Tradition
Sri Lanka

To my son Adam, born in May, 1985

Dear Adam,

As I begin this letter, I am aware that I cannot guarantee that I will be alive long enough to finish this first sentence. This points up a universal fact: ALL IS MYSTERY; WE KNOW ABSOLUTELY EVERYTHING ABOUT ABSOLUTELY NOTHING.

Before going further, on behalf of all human generations preceding yours, let me apologize to you and your generation for the wrongs we could have righted in the world you are inheriting from us. From time to time in human history, religious leaders have arisen to enlighten us, but we have inadequately heeded their counsel so that today we are faced with the possibility of the suicide of humanity through nuclear annihilation.

Yet it is not too late. Belatedly, aided by modern means of travel and communication, dialogue has begun on a world-wide scale so that we now speak of our planet, a speck in the cosmos, as a global village and the spaceship Earth. We are drawing from the religious heritages of the past as a living source of creative energy to bring new life, rather than premature death, to the human community.

Together we are engaged in the search for truth, indeed, for *the* Truth, God, who is the Author of all existence. All that is good and true is from the One God. The Christian tradition, whose roots are shared by those of the Jewish and Moslem faiths, teaches that there are two sources of knowledge—Creation and Revelation, both of which have the same Author, God. We learn not from one of the sources, but from both; not only from the world of which we are part, not only from scripture, but from both at the same time. Hence, we must be engaged in constant sharing with others, in true dialogue with all persons of all religions, sciences, and philosophies, for each can teach us something.

Christian tradition also teaches that perfect knowledge can be enjoyed only when we are face to face with God. The popular song line, "O Lord I want to see You," expresses this human yearning. In this life we have only imperfect knowledge; we never have the whole truth. Even in court each witness presents a different point of view. Our knowledge is imperfect regarding all existence, from the entire cosmos to the smallest particle, from our own life to that of the single-cell creature. ALL IS MYSTERY in this life. Our sisters and brothers of the Taoist, Confucianist, Zoroastrian, Primal, and other religions, as well as those who believe there is no God, will testify to this truth.

As a Christian, use your God-given intelligence and faith to the fullest. Develop a full, solid faith in the Word of God; cultivate an awareness of God at each moment. Nourish an intense love for God, yourself, and others.

The miracle of each moment is that the entire universe continues to exist, that each of our lives continues for one more moment. For the Christian, the greatest means of awareness of this fact, and of creative energy, is the Living Source of the Eucharist. The Eucharist penetrates most profoundly into the abiding mystery of existence and life; of matter and spirit; of the cosmos and our planet; of the totality of reality and *the* Reality, God; of the Creator and his creation; and most important, of God and God-become-one-of-us to reveal his saving love for all, a love which should be reflected in the lives of all Christians.

A privileged moment of awareness of existence and life is the moment of consecration in the Eucharistic celebration when, for the believing Christian, God sustains the existence of the universe for one more moment and changes bread and wine into the Body and Blood of the Resurrected Christ, God Incarnate. The appearance (*maya* ... Hinduism) of bread and wine remain, making the Eucharist the greatest *koan* (unsolvable by logical thinking . . . Buddhism), going beyond the mystery of quark symmetrics (modern physics).

A similar moment is the moment of Communion, when we receive the Risen Christ in the Eucharist, when life in its eternal dimensions is visibly given to us. This is a privileged moment of communion with God and with those who have already passed from this world to participate in the fullness of the Divine Presence, and with all our fellow human beings who at the same moment receive life from the same God, though not all may recognize that fact. Our communion is with God, the whole human community, and all creation. It is in this spirit, the Spirit of God, that we open ourselves to all others.

This, Adam, is the central legacy I wish to pass on to you. An awareness of the deep bond of love that exists between God, yourself, and all others is more precious than all the wealth of the world. With it, all has value and meaning. Without it, we are already dead.

Your father, Franklin G. O'Connor

Canada

Dear Niranjan,

I have not written to you before, but my recent conversation with your father prompted me to write this letter. First, let me congratulate you on winning the prestigious scholarship award for graduate studies in nuclear physics. I sincerely wish you a brilliant career in your chosen field of knowledge. Second, I was intrigued by the question you asked your father about the importance of religion in life and how it is that some take it for granted, while others question it or have deep reservations about it. Although your father suggested that I discuss the subject with you when you come home to spend your next vacation, I decided not to wait that long.

I presume that by the importance of religion, you mean faith in the scriptures. Every major religion has at least one scripture; the Hindus have too many of them. In most cases, this faith is created by the environment in which we spend our lives. From your childhood you have read and memorized many poems written by Tagore and others and have won several medals for reciting them in cultural functions. You have not only enjoyed and appreciated doing that, but in the process you have also developed faith in the poets' points of view on life. I once learned from an elderly man that during his childhood the favorite pastime of his close friend was to recite from the Bhagavad-gita, the most well-known Hindu scripture. The ideas contained in that book of seven hundred verses fascinated him so much that he developed a habit of chanting those verses throughout almost of his waking hours. He feels, and I agree, that very few of our activities need our total concentration and therefore, while performing our daily chores, we would be better off if we could force our wandering minds into some worthwhile thoughts.

You know what distinguishes a man from an animal. The

primary distinction among humans, however, lies in the quality of their thoughts. It is what we think that makes us happy or miserable. But in life's never-ending pursuit of happiness, we end up being miserable most of the time and we wonder why. The sages of yore discovered and loudly proclaimed that the fountain of eternal joy is not to be sought in the world outside; rather, it is within us all the time. If one is keen on attaining joy, there are several pathways from which to choose the one uniquely suitable to you. It is like your choosing nuclear physics as your field of specialization.

But our respective spheres of professional activity cannot, by themselves, raise us to the level of spiritual joy and fulfillment. Fortunately, we have inherited a treasure house of spiritual knowledge as well as the disciplines and practices to appreciate and live it. May I suggest that you take a peek at this treasure house and then decide for yourself. But as in any other discipline, you will be better off if you can find a teacher. A systematic study of the scriptures under the able guidance of an enlightened soul, and in company with other inquirers, is recommended by our predecessors.

But you may find such study impractical at this stage of your career. Nevertheless, your question goes deep and demands more than a cursory reply. As a starter, if you have not already done so, you may begin by reading the Bhagavad-gita, which has been translated and commented upon by many people. The translations are quite different in their approaches, and you may have to try several to find the one that you will like.

As you contemplate it, you will find that the essential nature of man is divine. Indeed, everything in creation is divine, and God is present everywhere. We have difficulty in perceiving Him because our mind is tainted with lust, greed, anger, and hatred. But we alone, of all created beings, have been given the power to get rid of these impurities and to manifest our divinity. Our religion is very practical. The scriptures tell us not merely about the goal but also about the means to attain it. Like those who have trod the path before us, we have the responsibility to follow, not only for our own sake, but also to be torchbearers for those who are yet to come.

More later.

>With love and best wishes,
>
>Mitra Uncle
>Atlanta, Georgia

P.S. See how the Hindus have developed the tradition of making divinity as explicit as possible. Take, for example, your name. It means "no blemishes." That is the example I see set before me when I call you by your name. Devout Hindus also chant appropriately designated verses glorifying the Lord as they undertake various activities during the day, including getting out of bed in the morning and retiring at night. Constant communion with God is the aim of this spiritual exercise.

Dear Young People,

All human beings, all animals, all plants, and all inorganic objects consist of character and form, of function and material. Although man is a material being *and* a spiritual one, he must be viewed as having a unified existence. It is wrong to perceive human beings from a bifurcated point of view.

Today it is necessary, however, to participate in the movement to reform man's spiritual life in order to remind him of his condition and to affirm the efforts that have been made to create the world anew—with goodness and with new moral values. To participate in such a movement of reformation, it is necessary to establish the center of goodness. Goodness means the practice of love, and God is the center of love. The seat of love is the heart, and the essence of God is the heart. Where there is heart there is life, and where there is life there is movement or creation, and creation always has a purpose.

The aim of creation is the experience of joy. This joy comes when created things, especially human beings, look toward God. And the response of human beings to God's love and creation is the aim of God. Life's plan is quite clear when we consider that man's purpose lies herein. Although modern science has been able to resemble God's creativity, it has not yet resembled the love of God. In order to resemble the love of God, we have to practice his love and live a life of goodness. Since the practice of love leads us to the manifestation of goodness itself, God, who is love, has to be regarded as the central standard of goodness. If we lived lives of goodness centered on God, world happiness and peace would be realized. But if we refuse to center our lives on God, we suffer pain and unhappiness.

With best wishes,

Kwan Soh Ko
Korea

To A Young Person:

My hair is grey,
My wrinkles are deep.
I discover, late, truths
I would I had grasped sooner.

Many will say to you
"Do that; go there;
This is what you should believe."
Obeying is easy,
Bringing security,
Enticing in a world so insecure.

My hope is for you
To adventure,
To look,
To listen,
To leave safe tracks,
To toss back and forth,
To find yourself.
But water your roots,
Hold the hand of a friend,
If only by a finger, a toe;
You will not be swept away.

You will discover your way:
The way for you,
You alone.
Live dangerously, excitingly.
Live life.

Live your life.
Live as yourself.

Jean Head

England

My dear son Bram,

From the Assembly of World Religions in McAfee, New Jersey, where about 850 delegates from eighty-five nations are meeting at the invitation of the Rev. Moon, let me take a few minutes to tell you about my personal hopes and dreams for the world you and your friends are and will be living in.

Although I miss you right now, I am immensely grateful to God for this time for reflection. I, like all men and women here, want to leave a world of peace and harmony for you where you will live a life of fulfillment. I admit that we in North America and Europe have been foolish and selfish in living a life of plenty in the face of global need. My prayer for you is that the earth will remain productive in your generation and that no one will blow up the globe with the arsenals my generation has been busy building up.

You know, son, I was born just three days after the first fatal bomb explosion in Japan—the very same day the peace treaty was signed. The world into which you were born is more potentially explosive but most definitely more resourceful. It took about two decades of my life to get into a highly competitive lifestyle—but you were born into it. I was a teenager when I learned about sex, politics, comics, and cartoons—but you were born into it. You surprised me a couple of weeks ago in your swimming class. At the age of nine, after a period of just two weeks of learning, you were swimming at the deep end! Your mother and I were very proud of you. Indeed, I have amazing confidence in you and all those intelligent, gifted, resourceful, blessed children of your generation. I truly hope that forty years from now, you will be sitting at a similar conference on peace and religious understanding and be able to write a similar note to your children and their children.

In the meantime, social, political, and religious structures will be changing—hopefully towards the goal of a more just society. Millions of people are now starving in what we call the third world (a term I dislike); that is, the developing nations of Asia, Africa, and South America. When I was a child, the tension was between the East and the West, but today it is between the North and the South. Polarities may change from decade to decade, but the poor have been with us throughout all these times. I hope there will be more redistribution of wealth in your world, more opportunities in the area of education, and more religious freedom for people to practice their faiths, no matter where they choose to live or no matter what their expression of God—Jesus, Muhammad, Krishna, Nanak, Gautama, or some other incarnation.

We are still novices at interreligious dialogue; we still deny freedom to others. I would ask you to share what you've inherited with others—men or women, believers or nonbelievers, black, brown, yellow, or white. That sharing includes your faith, your material blessings, and your wisdom, acquired from many sources, including your mother and me and a host of friends in Canada, India, and Singapore.

God bless, my son.

Your dad,

John T. Mathew, a minister in the United Church of Christ in Canada

Dear Youth,

Life is something like a game of cards, where the cards are shuffled according to the rules of the game. You yourself shuffle the cards and distribute them, but you cannot choose what is distributed; that is out of your control. But to play the game you do have free will. You can play any way you like. You can't choose the cards, but you can choose the method of playing. Destiny is something like the shuffled cards. You were born into a particular family, with a particular capacity, a particular body, in a particular environment and set of circumstances, with a specific intellectual, emotional, and physical capacity. When you play the game, you play to the best of your ability. Even if you lose, there is no regret because you have played to the best of your ability. And eventually a day may come when you win, whatever the cards.

So life gives us cards, and we play the game. Our particular cards constitute our destiny, and playing the game is an exercise of our free will.

How do you play the game best? That is where you get the help of the saints and sages, who have played the game and won. They will sit by your side and guide you in playing the game. Whatever the cards, do not grumble, because according to the rule of the game, you cannot choose your cards. You have shuffled your cards and distributed them yourself, and you are in a situation of your own making. You should concentrate on making the most out of your situation. Think wisely, act well, and try to win the game. Otherwise, you will be wasting all your energy in vain efforts. Do not waste your energy in grumbling, arguing, and complaining about your fate. You must accept the situation you are in. Such acceptance constitutes an important step in your spiritual life.

Sincerely,

V. Ramakrishnan
Singapore

My dearest Jimmy,

Now that you have successfully completed your education and will soon be returning home to participate actively in the working life in our country, I want to convey my heartiest congratulations to you on your splendid achievement. You have done well and we are proud of you.

You told me that many of your friends are interested in Buddhism and would like to know more about it. I have sent you some booklets printed by our organization, the Buddhist Missionary Society. I trust these booklets will make the Buddhist position clear to your friends.

In essence, Buddhism is a way of life. The Buddha-Dharma is a moral and philosophical system that expounds a unique path leading to emancipation and enlightenment. The simple but far-reaching advice given by the Buddha to his disciples is: "Do no evil"; "Do good"; and "Purify your mind." The last admonition is the most important piece of advice, for it is in man's mind that lust, hatred, greed, envy, egoism, deceit, and all forms of evil thoughts prevail. We are asked to subdue and kill all these passions of evil in our minds. This can be done by absorbing the teachings of the Buddha and by meditation. If man's mind is purified of all evil passions, he will be treading the path to enlightenment and he will be an asset—benefitting himself, society, and the country at large. An enlightened Buddhist is definitely a law-abiding and peaceful citizen of any country.

In our efforts to seek enlightenment, the Buddha exhorted us to practice patience, tolerance, and understanding in all our relationships with members of our family, our friends, and our spirutual companions. I feel that you must have put into practice these valued injunctions; otherwise, you would not have been able to cultivate so many new friends from diverse racial and religious denominations in a foreign country. Upon your return to our country, you should continue to uphold this particular aspect of our Buddha's teachings in order to assimilate yourself into our Malaysian society.

As you are aware, Malaysia is a multi-racial and multi-religious society and as such, it is of the utmost importance that everyone should put into practice the benign spirit of patience, tolerance, and understanding in their day-to-day dealings with one another. Even though Islam is the official religion of our country, practitioners of all the other religions—Christians, Hindus, Sikhs, Buddhists, Taoists, and Confucianists—are given absolute freedom to practice their respective religious beliefs and to perform their individual rites and rituals without any hindrance. Clause 11 of our constitution specifically states, "Every person has the right to profess and practice his religion." With this liberal provision in our constitution and the practice of patience, tolerance, and understanding, our country has lived in peace and harmony, with respect for diversity.

This interreligious harmony has created an atmosphere of intersocial collaboration. Thus if my Muslim friend celebrates his Hari Raya festival, it is obligatory on my part to send him a greeting card. In turn, my friend would invite me to his home to rejoice in his celebration and to partake of certain festival delicacies. Similarly, if my Christian or Hindu friends were to celebrate their religious festivals, I would extend the same courtesies to them and call at their homes to enjoy their festivities. However, when it comes to the celebration of our Chinese New Year, it is my turn to invite my Muslim, Christian, and Hindu friends to share with me in our rejoicings. Visits of such a nature promote interreligious friendship.

This tradition is a unique one, and I hope that, in due course, when you are in a position to assume the role of host, you will do your utmost to uphold and maintain this valued tradition by sharing with one another the joys and pleasures of our festive occasions, religious or otherwise. Friendship thus created should rise above race or religion. Through friendship and mutual understanding, we can build a harmonious, interracial, interreligious society, thus contributing to the peace and tranquility of our country and to the world at large.

As a Buddhist, I have a duty to respect and uphold our religion, but my advice to all my Buddhist friends is that, under no circumstances, should we, at any time, belittle, speak ill of, or look down upon another religion. All religions exist for the good of mankind. All religions exhort mankind to do good and to shun evil. We mut respect our friends of other religious denominations for what they are and for what they profess. Respect begets respect. If we expect others to respect us for what we are, we must reciprocate by respecting them for what they are. With respect, we gain friendship. With friendship, we gain peace and harmony.

I have been associated with our Buddhist movement, locally and internationally, for nearly forty years. As the President of the Buddhist Missionary Society since its inception in 1963, I have worked with leaders of other religious denominations promoting goodwill, friendship, and harmony in our multi-racial and multi-religious society in Kuala Lumpur. We have done our share to promote mutual understanding and mutual respect among the diverse religions. Since I have just passed the age of retirement and am now 78, I propose giving up the responsible positions that I am now holding to give way to younger leaders. That way I can have a real "retirement," hopping from one country to another for a relaxing holiday.

I close with my love and kindest regards to you.

Yours lovingly,

Teh Thean Choo
Kuala Lumpur, Malaysia

Dear Youth,

I have just participated in a very unique conference held at the Great Gorge Resort Center in McAfee, New Jersey. Representatives of all the major world religious traditions from eighty-five nations came together to dialogue and share. Called the First Assembly of the World's Religions, the conference included, among others, Hindus, Buddhists, Jews, Muslims, Taoists, Zoroastrians, Confucianists, and Christians of all denominations. Catholics, Episcopalians, Presbyterians, Baptists, Methodists, and members of the United Church of Christ were all present.

Even though individuals and nations differ greatly from each other, they are all expressions of Divine life; a Divine seed is planted in each one of us. Even though all religions have their own forms and rituals, there are many commonalities, and the end we all seek is pretty much the same.

The overall goal of the conference was to promote the search for world peace through basic understanding and unity and the elimination of violence. Peace cannot be attained, happiness cannot be achieved, and fulfillment cannot be found unless each individual cultivates the Divine presence, the Divine seed within us all. Because every single human being is religious, whether or not he or she realizes it, we all need to be in a relationship to a spiritual force, a creative process, a Divine presence.

One of the things that was most apparent at the conference was the possibility of unity in the midst of diversity or pluralism—whether it be diversity in the areas of belief, appearance, behavior, or social custom. The seed of unity planted at this conference can most certainly grow and one day produce a bountiful harvest.

Insensitivity to life—any form of life—will ultimately lead to insensitivity to all life. All life is sacred, and we are living in an era when creation itself is crying out, "Stop it!" to such insensitivity. If you are one of those who are sleeping while the world is coming apart at the seams; if God has given you the talent, the ability and the strength to act and you do nothing; if indeed you are perpetuating violence, even in a seemingly insignificant way, then you are bringing the same judgment on yourself as those who are actively participating in the destruction of the world. If you are not a part of the solution to the problem, then you are part of the problem. Remember, God is just! Your question should be the question the rich young ruler asked Jesus: "What shall we do to be saved?" Repent! Then give your life in the service of others and gain life, the best possible life, in return.

Do you really know how bad it is in your own back yard? Remember, no one is safe until everyone is safe. Your salvation depends on the salvation of others. Jesus knew how important this truth was. He spoke of this when he said, "I came not to be served but to serve and give my life in ransom for many—for the world."

As a servant, one occasionally gets tired. Jesus got tired and when he did, he would steal away and pray. But he would return restored, ready and willing to persevere.

My own call is to be a servant—a reconciling servant. To be a reconciler is risky. Ask the disciples of Jesus, ask Abe Lincoln, Gandhi, John F. Kennedy, Martin Luther King. I knew this danger existed before a cross was burned on my lawn, before a liquor bottle was thrown at my face.

Youth, whoever you are, wherever you are, God is calling you all to be a servant according to your talent. Above all else, answer that call. Say, like Isaiah the prophet, "Here am I, send me." God wants to use you in his creative process to save his world. I have definitely said yes. Join me and find life in all its fullness.

Blessings,

The Rev. Clifton V. Bullock, Pastor-Director
Washington Heights United Methodist Church
and Community Ministries
Battle Creek, Michigan

Dear Friends,

It is most natural for us all to want to live long, healthy, happy lives. We all strive toward this goal, but not just a few of us fail to achieve it. As we become increasingly frustrated and cynical, we ask ourselves, "Why are we failing?" Is this situation unalterable? Certainly not.

The secret of achievement is ambition in partnership with conviction. Conviction spurs one on towards right effort. To achieve anything in life, four factors are necessary: 1) the seed of ambition, 2) right effort, 3) time, and 4) the unknown factor of Divine Grace.

I once knew a young man who, from an early age, wanted to be a top executive. He promised himself that he would put forth his best efforts to achieve this goal. After he had completed his education, he landed a job as a salesman in a reputable company. He performed admirably, and when there was a call for a management trainee in the company, he confidently applied for the position. Although a number of competent trainees from well-respected companies were interviewed, this young man bagged the job. He continued to excel by going to night school to learn as much about the world of business as he could. Within a decade he had risen to a position of eminence within the firm. My friend's achievement was a direct result of ambition coupled with conviction.

Outer achievements alone, attained through ambition and conviction, do not guarantee happiness, however. Wisdom and inner strength bring peace of mind and will release us from impatience, despair, pride, overconfidence, anxiety, and self-aggrandizement. Wisdom and inner strength breed calmness, self-possession, and self-knowledge. Wisdom gives us the ability

to deal with dissolution as well as creation; it allows us to function as effective, happy, and free human beings.
Blessings on you.

Love,

Susheela Raghavan
Madras, India

Dear Samuel,

Greetings to you in the name of the Lord!

Since you are going away, I feel a responsibility to write you, to remind you of your legacy, and to encourage you to remain steadfast in the future.

Remember Jesus, He who is risen from the dead, who was and is and will be—the Eternal One. Keep Him as your Saviour and Redeemer!

You were born and reared in a Christian family, where you were taught the meaning of life, the reason for existence. You were also told that you are free to do as you please, but that you have duties and obligations.

You are now starting a new period of your life—but do not forget Jesus. Just as he was called to conquer death and rise again, you are being called to live as a child of God in the world and to accept the salvation of Christ.

In the midst of the confusion of this world—in the face of the contradictions of wealth and poverty—remember Jesus. Jesus said, "Seek ye first the kingdom of God and his righteousness—and all the rest will be given to you." Therefore, go wherever you want and do whatever your heart desires, but remember that one day you will stand before the judgment of God.

Jesus came to this earth to call us to be children of God and to reconcile us to God for eternity. Some day in the future you will be an active businessman, responsible for great numbers of people—Remember Jesus. He can guide you every step of your life. He can give you wisdom and freedom. He can guide you as you grow in many new directions.

Do not allow the world to co-opt you; stand firm. But you cannot stand on your own; only Jesus can help you. He said, "Peace I leave with you; my peace I give unto you; not as the world giveth give I unto you. Let not your heart be troubled; neither let it be afraid." (John 14:27)

Dear son, without the peace of the Lord Jesus and without the power of the Holy Spirit, you will never succeed, materially or spiritually. One day when you begin your family life, remember Jesus. He can help you choose the best person to be your partner, to live peacefully, with joy, guided by the Holy Spirit. Remember Jesus, and may the blessing of the Lord Jesus, the love of God, and the fellowship of the Spirit be with you always.

Most sincerely,

Your father, Kitan

My dear Srinivasan,

Cheers! I hope by now you have recovered from the stress and strain of your long, tedious journey from Delhi and are settling into your routine.

After I bade you farewell in the railway station, I luckily happened to witness on the platform something I wish to remember always. This incident was a fitting answer to your grumbling about our religious practices. Perhaps you may have forgotten our conversation and I had, too, except I was reminded by what I saw after your departure. I know you are already curious to know the incident and impatient with my circuitous way of revealing it. Let me straightaway come to the point.

The platform was exceedingly crowded at the time. Travellers, their friends, and relatives were hurriedly moving about, talking, shouting, and crying. Porters were dashingly driving the noisy carriers full of luggage. Railway announcements were adding to the commotion. In the midst of this almost intolerable din, on the dirty platform, a little ways away from all the commotion, sat an itinerant, ordinary *saadhu* on a deerskin mat, a small photo of Sri Vishnu in front of him. He was reciting the *Vishnu sahasranama*, completely unmindful of what was going on around him. I waited, watching until he completed the recitation. Not even for a second did he open his eyes, and there was absolutely no sign of any agitation because of the unspeakable degree of external disturbance. After the recitation, he quietly packed up his things, and within the next few minutes, he boarded a train.

Well, my friend, I recalled then our talk about our daily religious practice. In our present-day hurry and confusion, where is the time for the recitation or performance of the traditionally accepted religious texts or *puja*—at home or in the temple? We feel sorry for our hopeless and helpless situation. But in reality we forget the liberality of Hinduism. It is stated in every *puja* system and scriptures that if you do not have a convenient place and time and prescribed articles for your worship, don't fail to do your religious duty wherever and in whatever condition you are. God will be pleased with your sincerity of purpose. No time, place, or mode of being is perceived as unfavorable for worship. Lord Krishna exhorts: *"Patram, pushpam, phebam, tojam yo me bhaktya prayachhati. Jasyaaham bhaktynpahritam ashnami prayatabmanah."*

The above shining example of the *saadhu* speaks volumes about the religious liberality we have been graced with. Let us not find lame excuses for our failures in our duties. This is for our own good; where there is a will there is a way.

With pleasure,
Affectionately,

A. Pundara

Dear Young Men and Women,

As our future leaders, you will be shaping the course of humanity. I want you to know I have faith in you, for I believe you will learn from our mistakes. You will be wise and so will not commit the same errors and hold the same prejudices as my generation. I know that you will create a more harmonious, loving, and caring society, a society in which we will all coexist peacefully. You are our future, my dear little brothers and sisters. You have the marvellous gift of youthful energy. Utilize it for the benefit of our common humanity.

God bless you.

Sincerely,

Anil Sooklal
Durban, South Africa

Dear Young People,

Lord Buddha's teachings are often compared with a wish-fulfillment tree that has the ability to provide whatever a being desires. It was only after some years that I got a glimpse of the depth and complexity of the Suddbodharma—comparable to the depth, complexity, and richness of any human life—a mirror in which we learn about our own nature.

It would not be correct to stress one point of the teachings and not others, since I experience them as a perfect logical system in which each given answer supports other answers as well. It is not only through our intellect but also through our emotions that we grow. And Lord Buddha's compassion is felt by those who take sincere refuge in Him and his Dharma.

The different religions have different methods of helping their followers to find both temporal and ultimate happiness. Buddhism also has various ways, and all of them are centered in training the mind, which is where all action—physical or mental—is first generated.

There are several points I would like to share with you, as a part of today's younger generation:

First, even though most cultures highly emphasize the responsibility each person has for his own actions, there is not enough emphasis on the fact that each and every action produces a result which, in the short or long run, is going to be experienced. Each being is the creator of his or her own future—this is most important for young people to understand.

Second, we need to realize that human life is uncertain and temporal. A meditation on death may be helpful in keeping this earthly life in its true perspective.

Third, we often feel that we are the only ones who are undergoing stress and dissatisfaction, when, in fact, suffering is the nature of existence. If we could only realize this fact, we would become more compassionate toward others.

Fourth, everything that happens results from a particular cause or condition. We can choose to be positive rather than negative and thus generate goodwill and cooperation rather than ill will and competition. We must look inside ourselves, rather than outside, for the cause of whatever befalls us. If it ever becomes difficult for us to discern virtue from nonvirtue, we should seek the counsel of a wise teacher.

And finally, all major world religions have a code of conduct that has resulted from centuries of life experience, from centuries of discernment. It is the richness and validity of these religious traditions that provide the bedrock upon which one's spiritual (and material) world can be built. We should remember to cherish our heritage and never to take it for granted or abandon it.

With best wishes,

Julix Busto
Argentina

My dear Vandama,

In your letter you raised certain issues which are quite important in our day and age. Your curiosity regarding religion and its relevance for life is genuine. In responding to you, I would like to share the most important resources of my Hindu spiritual tradition.

Before doing so, I would like to discuss the meaning of religion, or Dharma. It is generally said that Hindu Dharma talks only about otherworldliness and has nothing to do with this world. The word *Dharma* is derived from the root *dhri*, which means "to uphold, to support." Dr. V. P. Kane, in his *History of Dharma*, Volume I, defines Dharma as: "1) the rights and duties of man as man; 2) his duties or privileges as a member of the community *aryam*." Dharma includes both rights and obligations, for rights cannot properly exist without corresponding obligations. Thus, Indian social ethics attempt to reconcile the ideals of liberty and equality through the concept of *svadharma* (one's own station).

The ultimate aim of life, according to all systems of Indian philosophy or religion, is to achieve *mokha* or liberation from all worldly pain and suffering, to achieve complete bliss. It can be achieved while living in this world as well as after death. *Samsura* (the world) is full of suffering, ignorance or *andya*, egoism or *asmita*, attachment or *raga*, aversion or *divesa*, clinging to life, and an instinctive fear of death. The bondage of the self is due to its wrong identification with worldly things. True liberation, therefore, means the end of this wrong identification through spiritual means such as knowledge, action, and faith or *bhakti*.

The main source of our spiritual tradition is the Upanishads, the Gita, and the Brahmsutra. The Upanishads are the concluding portion as well as the cream of the Vedas—the oldest extant literary works of the tradition. Some of the important Upanishads are: *Isha, Kena, Katha, Prashna, Mundaka, Mandukya, Taitlinya, Aitareya, Chhomdogya, Bradarnyaha*. Professor C. D. Sharma has rightly said that if one wants pearls, one has to dive deep into the ocean and contact the pebbles on the floor. These works are rightly regarded as the basis of all Indian philosophy. There is no important form of Hindu thought that is not rooted in the Upanishads.

I would wish for you and your generation to receive nourishment from reflection on these sacred books.

With love,

*Mohan Sharma
Rajasthan, India*

My dear Sons,

Your mother and I have always been careful to transmit to you the ethical and religious teachings of the major spiritual traditions of the world. We did so in a healthy attempt to teach you the virtues you will need throughout your life. Today's world is short of honest, virtuous, sincere, capable men and women with high moral principles.

We have tried—and it has not been an easy task—to educate you more through our actions and behavior than through mere words. We have attempted to develop your natural aptitudes and to serve as a model of a dignified, respectable life, full of happiness and reward.

I am sure you are not unaware that the world is now facing a painful, long-lasting crisis which contaminates everyone with its poison. As protection against this poison, we have, through daily family life, tried to transmit to you eternal values by pointing out God and his Son, Jesus Christ, as examples to which we may turn in critical times.

We have always denounced egoism, cynicism, and insensitivity, while trying to inculcate a belief in family, in country, and in the brotherhood of humanity. We are conscious of our imperfection and that at certain times we have failed in our noble mission as parents and educators. However, being aware of these failures, we did not evade our responsibility. The normal tensions and misunderstandings of family life should not diminish the importance of the teachings which we imparted to you. Small misunderstandings reveal the imperfection and weakness inherent in human beings. You must excuse and forgive them.

Of course we were not always able to demonstrate the importance of transcendental values and the marvel of a life dedicated to spiritual matters. However, God is a witness to our sincere intentions in this respect.

Another concern of ours has been to transmit to you a code of duties and obligations for you to follow, for life is a complex of obligations that are interconnected with the rules of justice and freedom. Thus we need to be concerned with truth, not only personally, but also globally. Only then will the current wave of disrespect and permissiveness be curtailed.

Above all, my dear sons, you must understand that the attainment of a better world results only from absolute compliance with God's laws. Without this compliance, we cannot fulfill our task in this world. We understand that it is not always easy and that we are not always willing or prepared to perceive God's will. However, a deep communion with Him is a powerful weapon against adversity and disillusionment. Furthermore, He is the only one who can really offer us a more complete and constructive life.

Alliance with God and a sense of his active presence in our lives will bring joy, humility, gratitude, and a sense of our mission in the world. May each of you experience a life filled with blessings, joy, and well-being.

With love,

Your father, Epitacio Torres
Porto Alegre, Brazil

Dear Youth,

As the generation of the future, you will be inheriting a world that is quite different from the one we live in now. But whatever form or shape this world will assume, in order to build a better society and to live creatively in it, you will have to be yourself and hold fast to your beliefs. Although you will need to have an unwavering faith in your own spiritual tradition, you will need simultaneously to respect the traditions of others and open yourself to dialogue and sharing with members of other faiths.

Sincerely,

Dohan Effendi
Indonesia

Dear Young Seeker,

Blessings!
I would like to convey to you my own experience in my search for God-consciousness. I was born into a Hindu family. My father had a Hindu background, but he had also been exposed to Christianity. He had been educated in a Christian mission school and had become a teacher in that same school. In my own spiritual practice, as I meditated on God's form as Shiva and also as Krishna, I experienced seeing light. Later on I experienced deep care and concern from my philosophy teacher, who was also a Methodist minister. He took me to Methodist services where I heard the lectures of many Christian ministers. In the Methodist Church, too, I experienced seeing light within. I began to feel that the Christ aspect of Jesus, like the Krisht aspect of Krishna, was Divine Light. Later on, whenever I attended services, whether in a synagogue, a church, a Sikh temple, or a Hindu temple, I felt the presence of God as light.
I came to realize that regardless of the name or the form of a religion, I could feel the presence of God. God is not the God only of Hindus or of Muslims or of Christians or of Jews, but of mankind, or, rather, of all the cosmos. His divinity, his indestructibility, his light is present in every living and nonliving being. The more I meditated on light, the more I began to feel love for all living beings. I cannot hate any person because I feel that God resides in everyone.
This has been my attitude and way of life. But you must find one form or expression of God according to your own background. Love that form and meditate through it on the Supreme Being.
"Love the Lord thy God with all thy strength, with all thy

heart, with all thy mind and with all thy soul." Then you will see God reflected in all human beings and you will realize that you love your neighbour as yourself. This experience will lift you up and enable you to live a harmonious, happy, healthy, and holy life.

Yours in the Supreme Being,

H. H. Dr. I. C. Sharma
Hoshiarpur, Punjab, India

Dear Friend,

The value of a heritage or a tradition cannot be adequately explained in a single letter or book because it is based on the accumulated experience of that tradition. Nevertheless, there is no such thing as an absolute value existing apart from any historical situation. Values depend on history; history and man depend on each other. To be human means to participate in history, and history, in the most general sense, is nothing but the story that man is continually telling himself about himself.

Thus an understanding of history is essential for today's youth! To understand history doesn't mean to know all the historical facts. The stuff you had to learn at high school doesn't bring much wisdom. To understand history means to understand the human situation which is the source of history, which is revealed continually through history, and which also constitutes your own situation. Once you have recognized this, you can investigate and understand what wise men had to say about this human situation.

Even as you engage in this process, it is important to realize that no wise man, no God, can think or believe for you. What you think or believe cannot be anything but your very own choice and responsibility. Therefore, evaluate your thoughts and beliefs critically; if you do not, you are merely borrowing someone else's thoughts and beliefs rather than formulating your own. The Buddha once said that one shouldn't accept something as the truth on any outside authority. He also said that no information can have eternal value. Investigate, therefore, with an open and attentive mind.

Finally, I would like to advise you to be true to the elements. Be true to the Earth: don't lose yourself in dreams, theories, or ideals, but restrict yourself to what can be done and to what is concrete.

Be true to the Water: don't consider yourself as a lone individual, but be aware that your very existence is part of a dynamic of interrelationships.

Be true to the Air: don't neglect your ideals; cultivate the freedom of your imagination.

Be true to the Fire: with anything you undertake, don't hold yourself back; don't be half-hearted, but immerse yourself in life without self-concern.

Be true to the Mind: cultivate your awareness in everything you do.

Finally, do not accept what I have written here without critical reflection. There is no inherent authority here, just advice from your friend, who wishes you happiness and wisdom.

Sincerely,

Erik

Dearest son Jesse,

I praise my God the Creator and my Saviour to be able to write you this very important letter. You know that I love you and I think of you constantly. At the Assembly of the World's Religions, I was asked, "What are the most important resources from your spiritual tradition, resources that have become the central legacy you wish to pass on to one young person you know?" It is essential that I share with you the basic foundation of my spiritual life so that you may be aware of the principle of life that circumstances and time can never change.

Your future stretches ahead of you in a world of problems, but God has an open door to give you the strength and the power you need to live a victorious life. Now you are in school studying and preparing yourself to meet the future. Bear in mind that you live in a world of cultural, racial, religious, educational, and economic diversity. I therefore appeal to you to live in humility and mutual understanding with those you encounter in your life. The Creator has given you the freedom of choice to live the way you like. You may live either negatively or positively. I would like to share with you a poem from an unknown author:

If a child lives with criticism, he learns to condemn;
If a child lives with hostility, he learns to fight;
If a child lives with ridicule, he learns to be shy.
If a child lives with jealousy, he learns to feel guilty.
If a child lives with tolerance, he learns to be patient;
If a child lives with encouragement, he learns to have confidence;
If a child lives with praise, he learns to appreciate;
If a child lives with fairness, he learns justice.
If a child lives with security, he learns to have faith;

If a child lives with approval, he learns to like himself;
If a child lives with acceptance and friendship, he finds love in the world.

May the Lord bless you, may you choose to live the right way.

Your father,

Gebre Michael Felema
Addis Ababa, Ethiopia

My dear Young People of the Future,

I write you, my dear young people who will come after us, because I want to pass on to you something of our tradition and experience. People have suffered greatly in the past because of their ignorance and covetousness. And although progress has been achieved as a result of the discoveries of science, which has brought us a better understanding of the laws of the universe, human suffering continues.

You will undoubtedly ask the same question that all men have asked: "Why do we live?"

We live because we want to live, because it is the law of life. To live is its own *raison d'être*.

"Why do we suffer?"

We suffer because we don't understand what is really good for us, because we live in a decadent society.

We observe that all beings are interdependent and live in a closed circle. Thus all beings, in order to be able to live, are obliged to eat one another in a perpetual change of form. In order to avoid certain suffering, we have to observe the laws of reason and righteousness. It seems that this is difficult to do, because human nature is passionate, greedy, hateful, and jealous. Man has difficulty understanding that only a way of righteousness and harmony is able to bring happiness.

As the trustees of the future, you will discover that one of your first priorities will be the study of science in order to develop your brain. Study to become a true man of science so you may understand better the laws of nature and be able to live in accordance with them. If you are a clever man, you will realize that wars never have brought happiness. Hate elicits hate. Be patient, subtle, and clever. A truly clever man will be a good man and will be able to avoid much pain and suffering. Be a deeply religious man, but don't be limited to a mere *credo*. True religion comes from the heart, not from the head. Be tolerant toward those who have a different opinion. Each man has his own particularities, his own orientation. It is not possible for all men to have the same conception of the universe at the same time. In the past, men suffered greatly from intolerance. Be tolerant of and compassionate toward all beings who suffer.

I would like to share with you a very simple religious practice I have. It is a Buddhist practice that everyone can participate in. First, sit down on a cushion, a *azfu*. Then cross your legs, stretch your spine, and push your head up. Hold your hands in a cosmic *mudra* in the same position as Sakyamuni, when he attained enlightenment.

When you begin *zazen*, you will probably find that all kinds of distracting thoughts begin to pop inside your head. It does not matter. Let them pass like a river, making no stop on the stones in their way. There will come a time when you will become quieter by yourself. Don't try to "get something." There is nothing to be grasped. The world is empty, without a permanent soul. It is nothing but energy. Be energy yourself. By this practice you will attain true liberty; you will become strong and quiet without having any aim to obtain. Only *zazen*. Try it. It is only in drinking water that we can appreciate its taste. Be glad and happy in the large and peaceful way of Buddhas and Bodhisattvas.

       Sincerely,

       The Rev. Teisen Perusat Stork, President
       The French Regional Center
       of the World Fellowship of Buddhists

> Go, go, always above, over above, o wisdom!
> Prajna Paramita Sutra

Dear Young Catholic,

There are many resources from our religious tradition that I would like to pass on to you, but I will concentrate on some central aspects of our own unique expression of spirituality.

First, I wish for you a sense of awe and wonder in approaching life. Our sacraments use symbols to celebrate both the ordinary and the extraordinary moments of our existence. Without a deep sense of the transcendent, one is unable to grasp the deeper, symbolic meaning which points beyond the limited scope of the here and now. This sense also nurtures the inner world of the spirit which is so neglected today. A person is uneasy with, even frightened of, his or her own thoughts and company if the world within, the *kingdom* within, is not developed. It is not surprising that so many people today rely totally on electronic means of stimulation when there is such disconnection from any real depth of personhood!

Second, I wish for a keen sense of your finiteness as a creature and thus a better perspective on your relationship with God. You are his *creature*, not his *creator*. Without this realization it is very difficult to be aware of the existence of sin and the dependence we have on God's grace to live above the simply human. Jesus has told us through the writings of the great saints that the glory of God is revealed in a person who is *fully* human, not merely human. Our society today does not acknowledge the existence of a conscience that answers to more than the demands of hedonism or pragmatism. A sense of sin and your own human limitation will deepen your awareness of your need for and dependence on a God-Father who loves you and calls you forth to be ever more than what you are today.

Finally, I share with you one of the greatest legacies of our faith, one held in common with other traditions—the Scriptures, the living Word of God. Within the pages of our Bible and most especially in the Gospels, God has made his plan for our salvation most clear to us. We do not just read about his love; we see it enfleshed in his Son who gave his life so that we might live eternally. The word of scripture can become formative, rather than just informative, if we *live* the Word as our religion encourages us to do. The Word becomes the content of our prayer and meditation, helping us to focus ever more clearly on the Word himself. Each year of your life, the scriptures will be nuanced by your life experiences, enabling you to have them resonate ever more deeply within you and point to the truth that their word is *real*.

It is extremely difficult to pass on an entire treasure in just a few gems, but if you accept what I bequeath to you, you yourself will be able to seek and find, to taste and see that goodness of the Lord which surpasses all human understanding.

In Christ Jesus,

Sister Frances Bernardone Kapouch, IHM

Dear son Raymond,

For us human beings, the relationship between two generations is not merely a perpetuation of the species. More important, it is the descendants' continuation of the Way to Happiness discovered and travelled by the ancestors. Therefore, a father must pass on to his children things he deems most invaluable. Nobody wants to see his wealth, whether it be material or spiritual, disappear from his own hands. Nobody wants to see his children or descendants live a less gratifying life than his own. But what is this "most invaluable thing?" If the older generation does not share the fruits of its life-long spiritual inquiry and provide guidance, then the younger generation cannot be freed from feeling its way through the darkness. Thus I am writing to tell you the spiritual resources in our tradition which I deem most important.

The Buddhist tradition consistently praises peace. Although in its historical development the Buddhist circle is divided into various sects, it never resorted to war as a means of dissolving disputes. Buddhists pursued the avenue of rational discussion. Even when Buddhism left India and spread to China, Tibet, Japan, Sri Lanka, and other Southeast Asian countries (and eventually Europe and America), it never caused bloodshed. Because of its rational attitude, Buddhism managed to coexist with indigenous religious and cultural traditions. There were times when Buddhists were persecuted and exiled, but they never resisted by armed force. In human history, Buddhism has been truly a religion that consistently carried out its ideal of peace.

That Buddhism is peaceful is doctrinally based. Because of its emphasis on viewing things "as they are," Buddhism can have an objective, open-minded attitude towards the tenets of other religions and philosophies. Hence it is sympathetic to the orientation of its opponents and can appreciate the value of mutually exclusive opinions. Here lies the doctrinal ground for sincerely respecting others. When it comes to practice, Buddhism advocates the Middle Path. It avoids extremes, advocates humility, and yields to others. In my experience, Buddhism is a religion consistent in both its doctrine and practice.

We now live in a pluralistic society where diverse convictions confront each other. If the human species is to be perpetuated, we must find a way for people of different races, cultures, persuasions, and convictions to live together peacefully. People have come to realize that tolerance is of the utmost importance to the peaceful coexistence of humankind. We must learn to respect others and to appreciate the manifestation of values different from our own. Sometimes, however, we cannot help submitting to the claim of superiority found in the sacred scriptures of almost all of our religious traditions. I am sure Buddhism can play a valuable role in forging an answer to the conflicts among world religions, on the practical as well as the theoretical level.

Your father,

Ton-heu Fok, President
The Dharmasthiti Buddhist Institute Ltd.
Hong Kong

Dear Young People,

No question in the world can be more important to me as an individual than this: "Why am I here and what am I expected to do with my life?"

This question implies that life is the most supreme blessing that one can ever receive. Unless you appreciate this gift above all others, your consciousness is not yet fully developed.

I wish to put before you an image to ponder. Each one of us comes into the world in a set of circumstances. *Circumstance* is a word derived from the Latin meaning "that which stands around" us. We may well call it a prison. Some prisons are less ugly than others, but all prisons (even those into which are born people with "a silver spoon in their mouth") may be perceived as irksome because they limit and stifle our freedom. We cannot change our prisons (the date and place of our birth, our parents, and other such *data* are fixed and immutable); but we can escape from the prison of circumstance. Indeed, as with prisoners of war, it is our duty to do so: a duty to ourselves that God graciously imposes upon each one of us.

We escape not by lulling ourselves in one way or another into daydreams, but by living our lives in such a way as to transcend the *effects* of our prison. Krishnamurti, in his early years, wrote a poem about a little bird that found itself imprisoned in a tree trunk. It clawed a little until it saw part of a green leaf, which it took to be the whole world; then as it saw the entire leaf it was sure that was the whole world. Then it clawed until it saw a whole sprig of leaves, then a whole branch, until at last, with bleeding feet, it clawed its way out of the tree trunk and flew away so that no longer could any prison hold it. That beautiful poem symbolizes what you and I must do in life to attain authentic freedom from the prison of circumstance into which we were born.

In my own Christian tradition the means of attaining freedom was expressed by Jesus: "You shall know the truth, and the truth shall make you free" (John 8:32). This process is usually long, arduous, and painful; the result, at every stage, is exhilarating and infinitely rewarding.

I have found that in this struggle I am surrounded by helpers from another dimension of being: angels, saints, sometimes my own relatives and other friends who have loved me and passed beyond this life, all being (in Hamlet's words) "ministers of grace." God as the source of all being uses such agents to help us, but each one of us must learn both to listen to such helpers and to work out our own salvation. We need and we receive grace to do so. Yet no agent can do our work for us. At most such agents are like computers; they can marvellously serve us and help us, but they cannot do what we have to do.

In our prayers to God many of us make specific requests for specific kinds of help. Our hearts are set on a particular job that we think is just what we need, or on a particular person that we think is the only person we could ever want to marry. Such prayers often go unanswered, as if God were deaf, and we may even doubt that he exists or that, if he does, he does not care. Then (it may be years or even decades later) we see how merciful and gracious God has been to us in *not* answering those prayers. How thankful we become that we did *not* get that position we thought at one time we wanted above all else or that we did *not* marry that person who seemed so essential to our happiness. The mills of God grind slowly indeed, but they grind to perfection. We can often see this truth even in this present life, which is, after all, only a very small slice of God's plan for our spiritual evolution.

Sincerely yours,

Geddes MacGregor
Los Angeles, California

My dear Young People,

I am sure you will grow up and live in a world far more advanced in the application of science and technology, and certainly far more complicated, than our world today. You will be surrounded by the marvels of an over-industrialized society, which will have everything to give you to increase your *joie de vivre*. The future that is awaiting you will be unparalleled in its capacity to provide material comforts to you.

But what you will not get from the civilization controlled by all the artifices of science and technology is the fulfillment of your total being as a person. To achieve this fulfillment, you will have to look to the profound, perennial message of your religious heritage, which will address you as an individual and teach you the lessons of interpersonal brotherhood.

Let me say what my own faith has taught me. It has taught me that all of us humans are expressions of the same divine principle, that we have to recognize this fact intensely, and that this recognition alone will act as the blinding force among us. What my religion wants me to be convinced of is that all the forces of disunity among men and women must be arrested to foster friendship, love, and understanding. Be what you are, but always remember (this is what my religion insists on) that, no matter what happens, all of us are images of the same divine God, and that unity among us all and the preservation of peace are the best prayer we can offer Him.

Yours lovingly,

R. A. *Sinari*

Dear Members of the Younger Generation,

My dear young people you are currently receiving an education that has a much greater emphasis on materialism than it does on the higher values of life. You may not realize the importance of spiritual values, but remember, a time will come when one becomes dissatisfied with only materialistic progress. Money is necessary in life, but it should not be the goal of one's life. It is a means to an end. Anyone who makes earning money the aim of life is in for frustration.

If you will remember to read the scriptures, you will find them a great solace and inspiration in times of difficulty. Whether it be the words of Christ, or the Buddha, or Krishna, or Moses, or Muhammad—their words are gems. You will find meditating on these words will help you to live a better, more purposeful life.

But remember, too, that a good and virtuous life is its own reward. When you help a fellow human being, not only is he or she happy, but you, too, feel a strange happiness. How can one be truly happy if his or her fellow beings are in misery? This is the message of the great masters, whose words are enshrined in the scriptures. The Unification Church has come to the forefront in our present day and age as the reviver of the great heritage of the spiritual masters. Do take time to read the great masters; they will offer you guidance and support.

My best wishes for your professional prosperity.

Sincerely,

Dr. Narayan H. Samtani
Varanasi, India

My dear Young Friends,

In this International Year of Youth, when we observe so many attempts to manipulate young people, I would like to open my heart to you and share some of my perceptions with you.

The first prerequisite to a life of integrity is a sincere, unflinching search for truth. Only the one who is ready to pay the price of loyalty to revealed truth is sincere. Only the one who does not allow himself to be contained by any limits in the search for truth is courageous. Today we live in an environment where the reality of eternal life is denied; if we earnestly desire eternal life, we must be like the young man in the Gospel who was willing to do anything to obtain it. In search of the truth we realize our limits and our possibilities. In pursuit of truth, we need teachers and leaders to show us the way to true life. If we are able to identify good teachers and leaders, we will find the basis of a life without disenchantment. How do I find truthful and good teachers and leaders? The answer to this question is found in the Gospel: "And he said to all, 'If anyone wants to come with me, he must forget himself, take up his cross every day, and follow me. For whoever wants to save his own life will lose it, but whoever loses his life for my sake will save it. Will a man gain anything if he wins the whole world but is himself lost or defeated? Of course not! If a man is ashamed of me and of my teaching, then the Son of Man will be ashamed of him when he comes in his glory and the glory of the Father and of the holy angels' " (Luke 9:23–26).

Jesus Christ came not to manipulate us but to redeem us and to lead us to find the true meaning of life. He said about himself, "I am the way, the truth, and the life" (John 14:6). The Resurrected One himself spoke words of truth when he announced, "I am the resurrection and the life; whoever believes in me will live, even though he dies; and whoever lives and believes in me will never die" (John 11:25–26).

God loves us so much that he sent us his Beloved Son, who, through his death on the Cross, fulfilled his mission to redeem us and called us to live the love of Almighty God. God has called us to love others and all of creation in the way he loved us in Jesus Christ, who said, "A new commandment I give you: love one another. As I have loved you, so you must love one another. If you have love for one another, then all will know that you are my disciples" (John 13:34–35).

The newness of this commandment consists of being called to love others as God loved us in Christ (Matt. 5:38–48). Jesus Christ reveals himself in every person in need of and awaiting our love. Jesus clearly proclaimed that at the Final Judgment we will be judged according to our fulfillment of the call to such love (Matt. 25:31–45). As you can see, the second condition of a "realized life" is love, which completes every justice and even surpasses it.

I am aware that many people do not believe in the possibility of such love. In their everyday lives, they believe only in the existence of egoistic love. The death of Jesus Christ, as well as his martyred followers (including St. Maximilian Kolbe, who gave his life for a fellow inmate in Auschwitz), not only shows the possibility of such a love, but actually demonstrates it.

I am personally convinced that the only prescription for a fulfilling, happy life is such a love, which makes of us a gift to God and to others. Such a love saves us, gives us strength, peace, and contentment. "A grain of wheat remains no more than a single grain unless it is dropped into the ground and dies. If it does die, then it produces many grains" (John 12:24).

Sincerely,

Walerian Skomka
Poland

Dearest Bobby,

This is an unsigned letter. You will know who I am as you read my letter. You will find me between the words and sentences. Read this letter carefully, especially the spaces between each word and sentence. In those spaces you will find me—and you will find yourself too. And you will remember me, Bobby.

Remember last Christmas when we were starting to put up decorations around the house? You suggested I buy some new decorations so that we didn't have to trouble ourselves with the old ones. But I insisted on digging through the attic, and together we made something out of all those old decorations. I still remember, Bobby, there were tears in your eyes as you fixed up Papa's old lantern, the one he made before he died. It was not only the Christmas decorations that made our house shine; it was the memories too.

Bobby, you used to throw peanuts into the little lake and watch how far the ripples went . . . Papa would say, "Don't preoccupy yourself with how far the ripples go out; instead watch where they come from." I still remember that you didn't understand him. Do you still remember when we were sitting on the shore of the beach one star-filled night, watching the ships passing by? I saw your eyes fixed on the ships' lights as they passed, one after the other. But you never noticed the beautiful light of the stars and the moon.

I don't know if you remember this, Bobby, but please try. When you were seven, I gave you a little plant. You asked me how this plant grew, and I told you that the roots would make it grow. You insisted on seeing the roots. But I told you that to uproot the plant could kill it. But you insisted; you were young and stubborn. Then I thought of a way to dig around the roots so that you could see them without killing the plant. And I did.

Bobby, there are other things I want to tell you. But this is what I want to tell you: You are growing . . . do not forget your roots . . . they are the source of your growth. Dig around the roots and when you see them, you will realize how beautiful growth is.

Don't fix your eyes on the light of the passing ships . . . but behold the fixed light of the stars. Bobby, you have wings to fly and you have roots . . . so that you cannot fly too high. Dig around the roots, Bobby. Begin today . . . Begin today by remembering . . . Do you remember, Bobby, do you remember?

Love,

(*Anonymous*)

My dear godson Adolfo,

Frankly, although I usually write effortlessly, I find it difficult to write this letter, not because I am unenthusiastic about its topic, but because I have never really quite thought of my faith and belief in Jesus Christ in terms that might make sense to a contemporary Filipino young person.

When I was on the verge of adolescence, I was sometimes upset by remarks made by some of my friends: "Wouldn't it be great if you hadn't been born a Catholic? Then you wouldn't have to worry about Sunday Mass, or no meat on Fridays, or Lent, or weekly confessions, or sexual inhibitions, or showing love and affection to your girlfriend." I was no holy Joe in high school, but I was a regular church-goer, and the only son in a one-parent family. My devout, widowed mother went to Mass every morning without fail, abstained from meat several days a week as an act of sacrifice (Tuesdays, for the poor souls in purgatory; Wednesdays, in honor of Saint Joseph; Fridays, in honor of the Passion of Christ; and Saturdays, in honor of Mary); always wore Saint Anthony's brown unless she had to attend a social function, and made it her personal apostolate to bring "lapsed" relatives back to the sacraments. But there were occasions when I felt it would have been better to be like the nominal Catholics next door in Quezon City; they were never really bothered by regular observances, especially those made mandatory by elders, church people, and the La Salle Brothers, under whom I went to school. All our obligations were imposed "under pain of sin," and our ears were assaulted by the fire and brimstone sermons of the Redemptorist priests who preached our annual three-day retreats.

Happily, a lot of these duties and burdens have been lifted from Roman Catholics, thanks to Vatican II and its renewed understanding of human nature and of the Christian message. No one says it openly, but obligations are no longer "under pain of sin," and many of the rules regarding fasting, abstinence, and sabbath rest have been relaxed. There is a much healthier attitude towards the joy of sex, and there is no longer any great insistence on confession for its own sake. The Church is still chauvinistic, however, and we have not solved the problem of power and authority, especially in the bureaucracy. And although there is much more genuine understanding of human sexuality, the official teachings indicate that the Church is still hung up on sex. I suppose this situation is a result of the fact that the members of the power elite are still celibates.

Since I myself have opted for a celibate lifestyle, what makes me happy about recent developments is that even celibacy by choice, independent of the sacramental ministry, has undergone a renewed understanding.

The healthiest development for the next generation of Catholics and for those who sympathize with our tradition is the lifting of the burden of a negative view of life and of human nature, in favor of a healthy joy in just being human. In its process of change, Catholicism has ceased to be identified with obligation, with rewards and punishments. Instead, it is being perceived as a tradition so wonderful that it can be shared with others without the use of coercion in any way.

What all Catholics share I would like to share with you of the next generation. We have had a long history of two thousand years. We have had our ups and downs and our fair share of failures, and things we didn't do quite right. But our tradition has somehow, in spite of these failures and shortcomings, managed to keep this vision clear: God so loved us that he gave us his continuing presence through all the wonderful things of life, through this planet and through the expanding universe. But in addition he has also set up his tent among us through being present to us in other human beings. We can also call on our brother Jesus, and with his help we can even dare to say, "Daddy" to that Someone who made all these things possible. I remember a significant statement of Albert Einstein's: "If there is a Power in the Universe, he is subtle but certainly not cruel." And this presence of God in Jesus, that is so intimate that we use the metaphor of a parent-child relationship, invites you and me and all our brothers and sisters everywhere—no matter their gender, race, beliefs, histories, or social class—into a communion. This is expressed in the communitarian metaphor of the Father, the Son, and the Spirit whom they have sent, who in turn enables us to say, "Father." The beauty of this is that we Christians share in this heightened awareness and look not so much for that which differentiates us from others as that which we have in common with other people and other traditions, histories, and beliefs.

If, indeed, we share this common vision of being one in the Transcendent, who made himself Immanent, then our common efforts at peace, nonviolence, and mutual understanding based on respecting each other's sensibilities and histories will bear fruit. And above all, our efforts to help each other and to make the treasures of our world available to all will make so much more sense. For in the giving of ourselves, we become more truly human. Our fondest wish is for a continuation of our life on this wonderful earth, a life beyond our physical death. Our hope is that death is not the end but nature's new beginning.

With great affection, I wish to share these thoughts with you.

Your ninong,

Andrew Gonzalez
Philippines

My dearest Daughters,

The Christian tradition has many words to express its beliefs and ideas, but it also has another language—its music, which is perhaps its richest heritage. In *The Idea of the Holy*, Rudolf Otto says that music can both evoke and express the *mysterium tremendum et fascinans*. We seem to underestimate and underuse this in our highly literate and wordy culture. Since you are musicians, I can ask you to treasure and pass on that heritage. Monteverdi took the poor and maimed from the streets of Venice and trained them to sing in St. Mark's as if they were angels. That story illustrates the transforming power of music, a power which is at the heart of religion, too. When Bach echoes through a Gothic cathedral, we know that God must be God. Mozart tells us not only of great longing but also of exquisite harmony. Beethoven arrives at joy in spite of war and deafness. Gregorian chant tells us of communal simplicity and stillness. The orthodox liturgy speaks of mystery and power. I could go on and on . . . the fellowship of the hymns of Wesley, the expression of Africa's vitality in the *Missa Luba*, the use of Indian *bhajons* and *nanjap*.

Keep the harmonies and the soaring scales in your hearts and use them with love for the good of the world.

Love,

Peggy Morgan
United Kingdom

Dear Rebecca,

As I promised, I will try to answer your question about my spiritual resources—resources from my religious tradition that have enabled me to live up to my Catholic faith, even under trying circumstances. As you must have deduced from attending Sunday School, receiving religious instruction and reading devotional materials, part of our Christian legacy is the Bible—that great book containing wisdom, counsel, prophecy, law, history, inspiration, and so much more. Second Timothy 3:15–16 says, "... know the holy scriptures, which are able to make thee wise unto salvation through faith, which is in Christ Jesus. All scripture is given by inspiration of God and is profitable for doctrine, for reproof, for correction, for instruction in righteousness ..."

The Bible is the backbone of my existence and from it I draw comfort, consolation, and guidance in dealing with the daily challenges that confront me. Since it is such a rich book, I would like to share some passages that have been helpful to me. But do not take my word for it; take time to read the Bible for yourself; allow it to speak to you directly.

Although we are called to perfection, we all experience many ups and downs in our lives that put our faith to the test. Our modern human dilemma is prefigured in the fall of Adam and Eve; the conflicts of Cain and Abel, and Esau and Jacob; and the trials of the chosen people journeying to the Promised Land. In the midst of tribulation, however, there is always a sign of hope: Abraham, Isaac, Moses, David, Jesus. Such signs confirm God's presence in our lives in times both of joy and of sorrow; whether we are good or bad. In Genesis 26:24 we read: "I am the God of your father Abraham. Do not be afraid. I am with you." Again, Exodus 34:7 tells us: The Lord is "a God merciful and gracious, slow to anger, and abounding in steadfast love and faithfulness . . ."

The Book of Proverbs is full of wise counsel: "Treasures wickedly come by give no benefit but right conduct brings delivery from death" (Proverbs 10:2). "He who loves discipline loves knowledge; stupid is the man who hates correction" (Proverbs 12:1). "Keep clear of the fool; you'll not find wise lips there" (Proverbs 14:17). "A good name is more desirable than great wealth; the respect of others is better than silver and gold" (Proverbs 22:1).

The Bible also speaks about the cycles and rhythms of life. There is a reason and a time to every purpose under heaven:

"A time to be born and a time to die, a time to plant, and a time to pluck up that which is planted.

A time to kill and a time to heal, a time to break down and a time to build up.

A time to weep and a time to laugh, a time to mourn and a time to dance . . .

A time to love and a time to hate, a time of war and a time of peace."

Ecclesiastes 3:1–8

Among the teachings of Jesus Christ which are a source of strength are the beatitudes. A verse from one of my favorite epistles also provides a great deal of nourishment: "Love is always patient and kind; it is never jealous; love is never boastful or conceited, it is never rude or selfish; it does not take offense and is not resentful; love takes no pleasure in other people's sins but delights in truth. It is always ready to excuse, to trust, to hope, and to endure whatever comes." By meditating on such passages, you will draw strength for your life, and you will develop clarity and wisdom. I would like to conclude this letter with a prayer an old woman once taught me:

* * *

O God, who created me in love, renew in me that same love that I may show in my life that love for you which our Lord Jesus Christ showed in his death for me. O God, show me the way, give me the light to know my true self, that in knowing it I may know you who are the Way, the Truth, and the Life. Amen.

Yours in faith,

Irene M. Kessy
Dar-es-Salaam, Tanzania